THE CRANBORNE CHASE PATH

Edward R Griffiths

A COMPLETE CIRCUIT OF CRANBORNE CHASE IN EASY STAGES WITH GUIDE MAPS AND SKETCHES

BY THE SAME AUTHOR

The Stour Valley Path   ISBN 0 9519376 1 8   Published 1994

"...the book is a gem which anybody..will add quickly
and gratefully to their bookshelf".......Dorset Life

First published - 1995

© EDWARD R GRIFFITHS

ISBN No 0 9519376 2 6

Published by Green Fields Books
13 Dalewood Avenue, Bear Cross
Bournemouth, BH11 9NR

CONTENTS

THE CRANBORNE CHASE PATH - ROUTE MAP

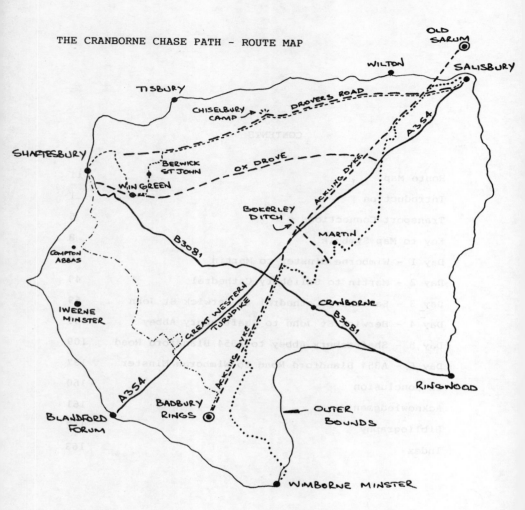

ROUTE 1 - WIMBORNE MINSTER TO SALISBURY CATHEDRAL:
SHOWN AS: ················

ROUTE 2 - SALISBURY CATHEDRAL TO SHAFTESBURY ABBEY:
SHOWN AS: ----·---·---·---

ROUTE 3 - SHAFTESBURY ABBEY TO WIMBORNE MINSTER:
SHOWN AS: ··--·---·-·--·-·

THE CRANBORNE CHASE PATH

INTRODUCTION

Cranborne Chase is a magical place. A place of enchantment, mystery and an enveloping beauty. It is England in microcosm - its history, its farming, its countryside and its animal and bird life - a land to be explored and savoured - all to the accompaniment of the song and clamour of innumerable birds, the rustling of the wind in countless trees and bushes and the busy, workday hum from many dairy and arable farms.

Cranborne Chase is unique whilst its variety demands intimate exploration. The downs and the valleys, the hidden villages and the different churches, the streams and country lanes all invite us to enjoy the peace of this old Royal hunting ground, the patronage of which resulted in a complete lack of anything approaching the size of a town anywhere within its boundaries. However, had the Great Western Turnpike not missed the central town of Cranborne when it was begun in 1755, the Chase would have become bisected by this major coach road in much the same way as it had been bisected by the Roman Ackling Dyke.

The only way to appreciate fully the beauty and intrigue that is Cranborne Chase is on foot. Fleeting glimpses through car or coach windows can offer no more than a fleeting enjoyment of anywhere - but especially so of Cranborne Chase.

Much of its treasures are hidden to the casual observer but a steady, unhurried walk can put you in touch with the paths and bridleways that have served those who have lived, worked or just passed through the Chase for thousands of years. This is quiet country where you can hear the birds singing and forget the hassles of everyday life - unless you are a farmer. In that case, I apologize for appearing to make the unforgivable, but usual, assumption that everything is fine and trouble-free because that's how it looks to refugees from the cities and towns of this fair land. On the other hand, I have yet to meet anyone who works in the countryside who would really like to live anywhere else.

However, to revert to my theme, this is a haven of peace where the air is clean and you feel remote. Yet, with this guide's recommended halts, you are never more than an hour's bus ride away from one of the three main towns which form the corners of our circuit. Yes, you can have a circuit of a triangular course - I've checked.

The Cranborne Chase Path is divided into three Stages of two days each and the many facets of the Chase are encapsulated within these Stages.

You may not choose to start at Wimborne as I did or even to go in the same anti-clockwise direction. Feel free! There can be no objection to personal preferences for start, finish or direction but I really must implore you, in the best interests of all the walkers who will come after you, and of all those who live and work on the Chase, not to deviate from the public

1

paths or bridleways and, when on farm tracks, to appreciate
that farmers, whilst generally happy to see passing visitors
enjoying their handiwork, are very busy and have more things
to do than to keep closing gates or ejecting trespassers from
land which does not have open access for all (See Page 142).
By all means, where there are multiple choices of paths on
your Ordnance Survey Map, choose your own at any time but keep
this special request in mind.

One of the major influences on the development of Cranborne
Chase was the arrival of the Romans who came via The Isle of
Wight in AD 45.   Vespasian's army conquered the local Dorset
inhabitants, the Durotriges, and based itself at Badbury Rings
which lies on the outer edge of what is now Cranborne Chase to
the North of Wimborne Minster.   From Badbury Rings, a network
of roads spread outwards to the harbour of Moriconium (now
Hamworthy, Poole), to the Iron Age hill fort of Maiden Castle
near Dorchester and, most important for our purposes, across
the Chase to Old Sarum - the hill fort which was finally
abandoned by the Romans' medieval successors in the 13th
Century in favour of a new riverside city - Salisbury.

The First Stage of our journey takes us through high farming
country and along a good length of the Ackling Dyke, the road
on a raised bank which the Romans built from Badbury Rings to
Old Sarum.   Whilst much of the Dyke is not easily recognizable
as Roman Road, some of it being in current use as farm tracks,
footpaths and even the A354, the majority of it still provides
easy and exhilerating walking across the Chase.

The Second Stage, from Salisbury to Shaftesbury Abbey carries
us along the high downs on the Drovers' Road and the Ox Drove,
both of which were used by drovers and farmers bringing their
cattle to Salisbury market along these relatively dry tracks -
the valley plains of the Rivers Nadder and Ebble on either
side being virtually impassable for most of the year.

The Third Stage takes us over high downland and through deep
valleys where cattle have grazed and crops have been planted
since time immemorial.   On this Stage, we stay mainly on high
ground, including our long-awaited visit to Badbury Rings,
before the final descent into Wimborne and journey's end.

Further information is given in each Stage's introduction and,
as points of special interest are approached along the way,
more details are given in the accompanying text.

To plan your expeditions you will need to obtain copies of the
Wilts and Dorset red timetables for routes between the major
towns and villages but, for the rural services, you should get
copies of "Public Transport in Rural Dorset", issued in
separate parts for different central towns, by Dorset County
Council and is available from Tourist Information Centres or
direct from County Hall, Dorchester.   The Stage maps are very
detailed but they are not to scale.   They should be used in
conjunction with Ordnance Survey Landranger maps Nos. 184, 195

and 183 in that order - (if you're going anti-clockwise, that is). The sketch maps in this guide are probably the most detailed that you will come across but they do not usually cover more than a few yards either side of our path so, if you wander off to view something or even manage to get lost, you may need the Ordnance Survey maps to find your way back onto the proper route.

As already mentioned, the Cranborne Chase Path is divided into six days with an average length of 12.66 miles each, although this varies to suit convenient stopping places approximately half way between our major towns. Each day is further broken down into shorter sections, some no more than 3/4 mile long. There is a "Transport Connections" section which shows where a car may park to drop you off or to wait for you at the end of the day. Bus connections at the beginning and end of each day are also shown although, obviously, times of buses cannot be included and these must be checked with your timetables.

My own preference is to park the car near the end of the Day's walk, catch the earliest bus to the start and walk back to the car. This way, it doesn't matter how long you take over your journey and it leaves you free to stop and stare - after all, it's not meant to be a route march. However, one plea from me on behalf of all beleagured landlords and landladies, and not only here on the Chase. Don't just park in the most convenient pub car park and abandon your car for the day, even if you intend indulging in the most expensive meal on the menu when you get back. Ask for permission first. You will more often than not be made welcome but it isn't unknown for a pub car park to be filled by organized rambling groups for an entire day, only for a mass exodus to occur, with little or no custom for the inn, at the end of the day.

Now, experienced walkers should not need reminding but, although the Country Code is already well known , there are definitions and guidelines concerning Rights of Way which are not so well known and need to be fully understood before you venture out into open country and across farmland.

If you find a gate open, leave it open but otherwise you must always close gates behind you. We are only visitors in the countryside, especially in arable and pasture land. Take care of it, don't drop litter and respect the privacy of those whose doors you go past.

Apart from that, specific Acts need to be reinforced so that those who follow in our footsteps will have a good example to follow, as well.

Signposting and Waymarking:
The County Council only has to erect and maintain signposts where a Public Right of Way actually leaves a metalled (tarmac) road. Additionally, the County Council has the power to Waymark paths where the route is not obvious - but it doesn't have an obligation to do so.

Stiles and gates have to be maintained by the landowner where they cross Public Footpaths - "to the standard of repair required to prevent unreasonable interference with the rights of the person using the footpath or bridleway" - Section 28, Countryside Act 1968.

Paths through fields:
Under the Rights of Way Act 1990, if a path follows the edge of a field, the surface must not be ploughed or disturbed, The law requires a minimum width of 1.5 metres for a footpath and 2.5 metres for a bridleway at the edge of a field.
If a path crosses a field or enclosure, the path must be reinstated within 14 days of ploughing to a minimum width of 1 metre for a footpath and 2 metres for a bridleway.

Obstruction or loss of path:
The County Council recommends that, when faced with an obstruction on the correct route i.e. lack of stiles, gates or exits from fields, you should make a slight deviation and report the obstruction to the Footpaths Liaison Officer of the Parish in which the obstruction occurs or to the Rights of Way Section of the County Council - they are always keen to help. Further, such obstructions are illegal under Section 137 of the 1980 Highways Act.

By the way, under Section 59 of the Wildlife and Countryside Act of 1981, a bull may not be released into a field or enclosure crossed by a Right of Way unless it is less than ten months old or, if older, accompanied by cows or heifers. If you come across a bull with eleven or more cows with him, you should be safe. Apparently, eleven is the magic figure which leaves the bull insufficient energy to bother with hikers.

One last request - Many English villages have lost, or are in danger of losing, their local village shop and post office due to lack of custom, with inhabitants working outside the village or only living there at weekends. We can all help to keep this important part of the life and culture of rural England by giving these shops our custom as we pass by. Take the time to call into every village store that you can (there aren't that many on this walk) and buy a few provisions, a drink or anything that you would need to get the next time you are due to visit your local Supermarket. Every little helps.

Now, wearing a good, stout pair of hiking boots and carrying enough waterproofs to protect you against any sudden changes in weather whilst you are stranded in the depths of the country, it's time to set out. Off you go and enjoy yourself! I wish I was coming with you.

THE CRANBORNE CHASE PATH - TRANSPORT CONNECTIONS

Car parking suggestions are made purely on the assumption that cars will only be parked after careful consideration for other users of lanes, verges and gateways.

Buses are all Wilts and Dorset buses unless marked *. These are not daily and are irregular- Check "Rural" timetables.

DAY 1 STAGES:

	STAGE MILES	CAR STOPS	BUS STOPS
1	0	Wimborne Car Parks	X13 132 133 139 The Square
2	-	- ditto -	X13 132 133 139
3	-	nil	nil
4	3	On verges - with care	nil
5	4.25	Near Bradford Barrow - with care	nil
6	5.50	Near Witchampton Church	182* 250* 300 319
7	5.50	- ditto -	182* 250* 300 319
8	7.50	Manswood or Moor Crichel	182* at Manswood + 300 319
9	8	Holly Grove - with care	nil
10	8.75	Ackling Dyke Lay-by	300 403* at Gussages
11	11	Monkton Lane/Dyke junction	403* at Monkton
12	12	B3081 wide verges	184 185 323* 400* Handley X
13	13.50	- ditto -	184 185 400*Yew Tree Garage
14	14	Pentridge Village (limited)	184 185 400* at A354
15	-	nil	nil
16	17	Martin Down Car Park	nil
17	17.75	- ditto - and at Martin (past East Martin turn)	184 185 323* 400* Coote Arms 400* Martin (E. Martin turn) 42 Martin (Townsend)

DAY 2 STAGES

STAGE MILES		CAR STOPS	BUS STOPS
1	0	Martin (past East Martin turn)	184 185 323* 400* Coote Arms 400* Martin (E. Martin turn) 42 Martin (Townsend)
2	-	nil	nil
3	3.50	A354 Lay-bys, with care	184 185 by request at suitable stops
4	6.25	Lay-by at Ackling Dyke	29 at X-roads (request)
5	7.25	On R/Course lane, with care	nil
6	8.50	On A3094, with care	Can't find any, but there's a lay-by by the Golf Course
7	9.50	In West Harnham	nil
8	11	Mill Road Car Park) Cathedral Car Park) City Centre Car Parks)	184 185 323* 400* 42 29

DAY 3 STAGES

STAGE MILES		CAR STOPS	BUS STOPS
1	0	Mill Road Car Park) Cathedral Car Park) City Centre Car Parks)	29 for all villages on the Ebble valley side. 27 for all villages on the A30 15 as far as Ludwell and 26 as far as Swallowcliffe.
2	1.50	nil	184 185 on A354
3	3.25	On R/Course lane, with care	- ditto -
4	3.75 4 4.75	Near Racecourse) Harewarren Lay-By) 2nd Harewarren Lay-By)	- ditto -
5	-	nil	- ditto -
6	10.25	By-Way near Fovant Hut	- ditto -
7	13.25	Lay-By near Alvediston Road	- ditto -
8	-	nil	On A30 down Whitesheet Hill
9	15.50	Berwick St John Lay-By, with full consideration)	29 only-to Salisbury or Shaftesbury

DAY 4 STAGES

STAGE MILES		CAR STOPS	BUS STOPS
1	0	Berwick St John Lay-By, with) full consideration)	29 from Shaftesbury
2	1.50	By-Way near Ludwell Road corner	nil
3	2.50	Win Green Car Park	nil
4	-	nil	nil
5	4.50 4.75	Off the A30 if you're lucky and) Near Ludwell 1st School)	29 and 26/27
6	-	Hardly - Lanes are too narrow	nil
7	-	nil	nil
8/9	8	Coppice Lane Car Park	29,26/27,X13,139

DAY 5 STAGES

1	0	Shaftesbury - any Car Park	29,X13,139,401*
2	-	nil	nil
3	2.25	Lay-By nr Cann Village Hall	X13,139,401*
4	-	nil	401*
5	3.75	Melbury Down Car Park & Lay-Bys	nil
6	5.50	Off Map at Ashmore - near pond	400*,401*
7	5.50	Ashmore - near pond	400*,401*
8	-	nil	nil
9	-	nil	nil
10	9.25	Tarrant Gunville Church	323*,403*
11	9.50	School Close - thoughtfully	323*,403*
CD	11.25	Chettle - if you have a Caravan	nil
12	12/13	A354 near gate - only 1 car) OR Lay-By towards Tarrant Hinton) OR in Tarrant Hinton, with care)	184,323*

DAY 6 STAGES

STAGE MILES		CAR STOPS	BUS STOPS
1	0	A354 near gate - only 1 car) OR Lay-By towards Tarrant Hinton) OR in Tarrant Hinton, with care)	184,323*
2	-	nil	nil
3	-	nil	nil
4	4.25	On Witchampton road/Hemsworth Farm	nil
5	-	nil	nil
6	6.50	Badbury Rings Car Park	nil
7	6.50 7	Badbury Rings Car Park and) B3082 Car Park in Beech Avenue)	nil
8	-	nil	nil
9	9	South Lodge Car Park	nil
10	9.75	Pamphill Green Car Park	nil
11	11 11.25	Old Road Pay & Displays) OR Wimborne Car Parks)	X13,139,333*

The Wilts and Dorset timetables and the "Public Transport in Rural Dorset" timetables are now published in separate parts and you should collect these from Tourist Information Centres before planning your walks. This, together with poring over the Guide Maps and Ordnance Survey Maps, is very much part of the fun of a great exploration.

KEY TO SKETCH MAP SYMBOLS

ROUTE	` ---- ------- `	HEDGE	
WIRE FENCE		WOOD/IRON FENCE	
STILE		GATES, LARGE/SMALL	
SOLID WALL		BRIDGE OVER STREAM	
DECIDUOUS TREE		FIR TREE	
SPECIFIC BUILDING		VARIOUS BUILDINGS	
EMBANKMENT		OVERHEAD WIRES	
RIVER/STREAM		FOOTPATH/B'WAY SIGN	
ADJOINING MAP NO.		MILES FROM START	

DAY 1 INTRODUCTION

Wimborne Minster to Martin

From the Minster Church of St Cuthburga, this First Day's walk
takes you into the agricultural and dairy heartland of
Cranborne Chase, passing within a few miles of Cranborne
itself.   You pass along ancient tracks and the Roman Ackling
Dyke.   You cross over the Bronze age Dorset Cursus and visit
a couple of fine churches before arriving at Martin to finish
your first Day.   There are some spooky goings-on today, but
don't concern yourself just yet.   Oh, and you need O S Maps
Nos 195 and 184.

	STAGE	MILES	TOTAL
1	Wimborne Minster to Walford	0.50	0.50
2	Walford to Catley Copse	0.75	1.25
3	Catley Copse to High Hall	0.75	2
4	High Hall to Barnsley Lane	1	3
5	Barnsley Lane to Bradford Barrow	1.25	4.25
6	Bradford Barrow to Witchampton	1.25	5.50
7	Witchampton to Manswood Lane	1	6.50
8	Manswood Lane to Cock Road Woods	1.25	7.75
9	Cock Road Woods to Sovell Down	1.00	8.75
10	Sovell Down to Harley Wood	1.25	10
11	Harley Wood to Wyke Down	1.50	11.50
12	Wyke Down to Bottlebush Down	1	12.50
13	Bottlebush Down to Cursus Gate	0.75	13.25
14	Cursus Gate to Pentridge Hill	1	14.25
15	Pentridge Hill	1	15.25
16	Pentridge Hill to Bokerley Ditch	1	16.25
17	Bokerley Ditch to Martin	1.50	17.75

If you wish, you can finish Day 1 early, at Bottlebush Down in
12.1/2 miles. This will leave you 5 miles further to walk on
Day 2 but an early break might be welcome.

By the way, each Day is meant to be a walk-and-learn exercise
so pay attention to the text. I'll be asking questions later.

DAY 1 - STAGE 1

Wimborne Minster to Walford

As our venture onto The Royal Chase Path starts by the North
porch of the Minster Church of St Cuthburga, it would behove
us all to go into the Minster before moving off. However, as
you will be starting very early on this longest Day, it will
be best if you wait until the very end of your journey around
Cranborne Chase so that you may enjoy a more relaxed, and
possibly, celebratory visit. So, with your back to the glass
porch doors and your own personal target ahead of you, it's
time to set out on a truly great adventure.

Out of the churchyard gates, cross over paved Cooks Row and,
passing the conveniences under the trees, continue across
Cornmarket into Church Street.

Whilst viewing some of Wimborne Minster (the town), you may
wish to make a mental note of a suitable watering hole for
your triumphal return. The first of these, Oddfellows Arms,
is now on your right, whilst your short walk out of town takes
you past The King's Head Hotel and Quinney's, where you can
find a rewarding pot of tea and a selection of fabulous cakes.

At the intersection of West Street with Wimborne Square, cross
on the pedestrian crossing and go past The King's Head. If
you want to leave the traffic already, you can divert up West
Street to Redcotts Lane on the right - then follow it, and its
continuing footpaths, all the way to Blind Lane and Walford
Mill where you can rejoin the rest of us.

Straight on, along West Borough, you will pass Quinney's and,
almost opposite, the revitalized Tivoli Cinema. This was
originally a fine 18th Century house until it was converted
into a cinema in the 1930's. It was abandoned in the 1970's
and restored in 1993 - 1994 by the Tivoli Trust.

After the traffic lights, Wimborne Town Councils' Offices and
School Lane on your left, cross over to the RH side of the
road as the pavement runs out on your side. Then, passing
Chapel Lane and the traffic lights at the Stone Lane junction,
cross over East Borough to Walford Bridge under which flows
the River Allen which you will meet several times today.

Opposite East Borough is Knobcrook Lane and the Walford Mill
Craft Centre which was established by the Dorset Craft Guild.
This is a converted 18th Century flour mill, where you could
spend many hours admiring the ever-changing exhibitions of
designs of invited Dorset craftsmen and women and the works of
the resident artists and designers of textiles, ceramics,
wood, jewellery, glass and metalwork.

Now, cross over the bridge over the River Allen and continue,
out of Wimborne, passing the Crown and Anchor Inn on the other
side of the road.

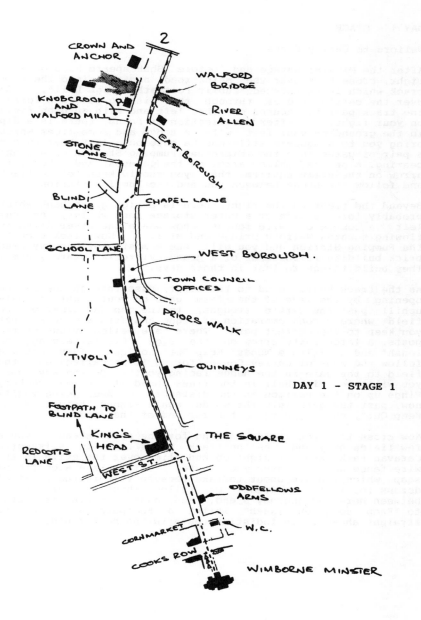

CROWN AND ANCHOR

2

WALFORD BRIDGE

KNOBCROOK AND WALFORD MILL

P

RIVER ALLEN

STONE LANE

EAST BOROUGH

BLIND LANE

CHAPEL LANE

SCHOOL LANE

WEST BOROUGH.

TOWN COUNCIL OFFICES

PRIORS WALK

'TIVOLI'

QUINNEYS

DAY 1 - STAGE 1

FOOTPATH TO BLIND LANE

KING'S HEAD

THE SQUARE

REDCOTTS LANE

WEST ST.

ODDFELLOWS ARMS

W.C.

CORNMARKET

COOKS ROW

WIMBORNE MINSTER

DAY 1 - STAGE 2

Walford to Catley Copse

After the Minster Garage and before Shakespeare Road on your
right, cross back over the main road and turn into the farm
track which is signposted "Public Footpath - High Hall". Go
over the cattle grid or through the kissing gate and follow
the track past two houses on the left and with an open field
on your right. After a collection of barns, there is a dip
in the ground on your left with a hedge and some trees which
bring you to a squeeze stile and a gate on a left bearing and
a pair of gates into the Wimborne Pumping Station on a right
bearing. A painted yellow arrow on the gatepost and a Footpath
arrow on the stile confirm that you should keep to the track
and follow the hedge between you and the Pumping Station.

Beyond the trees on the right there is a high grass bank which
probably forms a side of a water storage tank whilst, on your
left, a couple of wire fences show where the River Allen is
flowing towards Walford Bridge and Mill. Now, look back to
the Pumping Station and you will see a most glorious ivy-clad
brick building reminiscent of a grand Victorian stately home.
They built things to last in those days.

As the track bears round to the right, pass through the narrow
opening by the side of the farm gate on your right and walk
uphill, past the cattle troughs, to the top RH corner of the
field where a conglomeration of signs and arrows ensures that
you keep to the correct path. There are yellow arrows on two
posts, a large white arrow on the sign "Please keep dogs on
leash" and a "Private Woods Keep Out" notice. Turn left and
follow the edge of Catley Copse (for so it is called) down the
field to the gate in the hedge facing you. On the way down,
you will see High Hall in the trees ahead of you and Badbury
Rings up on the horizon in the distance. Keep going uphill
now, past the gate into the woods, again signed "Private Woods
Keep Out", until you reach the far end of the woods.

Now cross the open field, aiming for the pylon ahead of you a
few fields away and, as the track bears right to Wilksworth
Caravan Park, keep straight on and climb over the stile in the
wire fence which crosses your route. This is a significant
step which you are about to take because this is the first of
dozens (or is it hundreds) of stiles which you will cross
between here and journey's end. And, again, we are instructed
to "Keep dogs on leash" whilst a Footpath arrow points
straight ahead to an indistinct path in the next field.

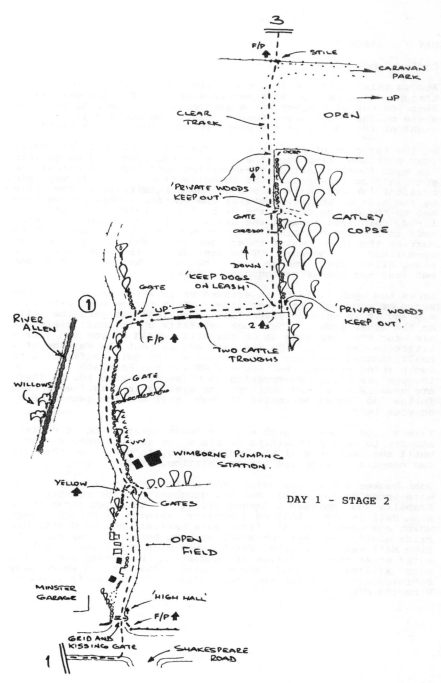

DAY 1 - STAGE 2

13

DAY 1 - STAGE 3

Catley Copse to High Hall

Across this field, climb over the stile into a small wood
through which runs a two-sleepers wide by 50ft long walkway to
keep you out of the bog which graces it.   Stepping over the
stile on the other side, keep straight on and aim just to the
right of the RH leg of the electricity pylon in this field.

On the far side of the field, cross the track which straddles
your path and climb over the stile in the fence and hedge into
the next field.   All of these stiles have Footpath arrows, so
you can't be in any doubt of the direction.   Anyway, aim
straight for High Hall as you go down this field to the stile
by the side of the farm gate at the bottom.   More arrows here
and on the bridge across the River Allen, which is in the next
field, point you towards the Hall.   Follow the fence on your
left to the end of this field, going over a brick tunnel which
carries the ditch water under your path, and go into the next
open field.   (Be sure NOT to veer off to the right after the
River Allen bridge and go over the ditch bridge - I did, got
wet feet and became surrounded by cows.)

Cross the open field to an arrowed stile which leads into the
strip of woods on the other side.   This narrow wood sits in a
dip and it is only 35 yards until you leave it over the stile
on the other side.   Now, look carefully up the next field and
aim for the farm gate up on the hill ahead of you and just a
little to the left.   On the way, you go past the RH edge of a
small, fenced wood and your arrival at the gate confirms, with
two painted arrows, that you are OK for the Footpath.   Go
through the gate, remembering to close it behind you as there
are usually some very smart ponies grazing in this field, and
follow the fenced perimeter of High Hall and the tennis court
on your left.

Take a close look at High Hall, without trespassing of course,
and try to retain something of its style in your memory - only
until the last Day of the last Section, though - so that you
can compare it with its bigger relation, Kingston Lacy.

John Bankes had a son, Ralph who built Kingston Lacy (of which
more later on the walk), and six daughters.   The youngest was
Arabella who married a Samuel Gilly.   This gentleman built
High Hall in about 1670 as a smaller version of Kingston Lacy
which was completed only five years earlier and, no doubt, his
bride would have felt instantly at home here.   By descent,
High Hall passed to John Fitch who made a fortune in public
works after the Great Fire of London.   He passed his skills
onto William, his son, who was also a builder and whose many
achievements included the construction of the South aisle of
Wimborne Minster.

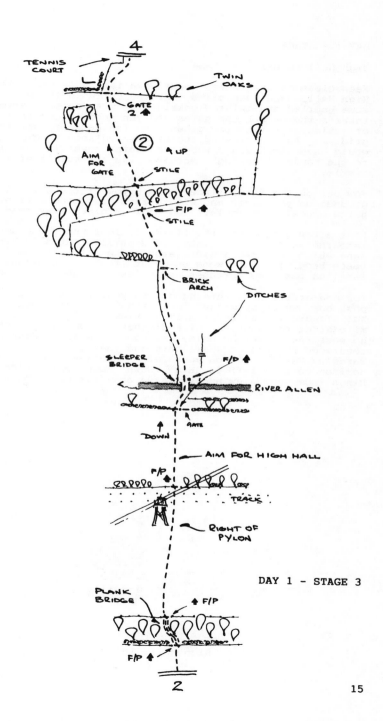

4

TWIN OAKS

GATE 2

2

AIM FOR GATE

4 UP

STILE

F/P

STILE

BRICK ARCH

DITCHES

SLEEPER BRIDGE

F/D

RIVER ALLEN

GATE

DOWN

AIM FOR HIGH HALL

F/P

TRACK

RIGHT OF PYLON

DAY 1 - STAGE 3

PLANK BRIDGE

F/P

F/P

2

DAY 1 - STAGE 4

High Hall to Barnsley Lane

Keep close to the fence, passing a farm gate which leads into
High Hall, and then climb over the stile in the wire fence by
some gnarled and twisted oaks.   A Footpath arrow points
towards the main house gates and you need to continue in this
direction, leaving the grounds by the gate or over the cattle
grid.   As you crossed the stile, a glance towards the house
would have shown you a wood-clad water tower in the trees near
to the house, looking something like the turret of a Bavarian
castle.

Now out on the tarmac lane, with a row of trees in High Hall's
grounds on your left and with a farm track and a triplicity of
gates opposite, turn left and begin a nice, easy road walk.

Past a few gates into the fields to left and right and a track
into the wood on the right, you arrive at a RH bend in the
lane which acquires a wide verge and a ditch on the left and a
beech hedge into the wood on your right.   Continuing up the
lane, go past two cottages and a few more gates in the hedges.

You now arrive at a turning off to your right, just opposite a
post box, which is signed for "Barnsley Farm".   Don't turn off
but prepare yourself for a long, slow uphill walk of about 3/4
mile along the lane.   With ditches and verges on both sides,
go past the Lower Barnsley Cottages, Barnsley House with its
tennis court, past a small barn and the turning off to "Lower
Barnsley Farm" - all on your left - and keep going.   Up on the
horizon to your left is King Down Wood which hides Badbury
Rings from your view and you have open fields on both sides.

High Hall. This Page

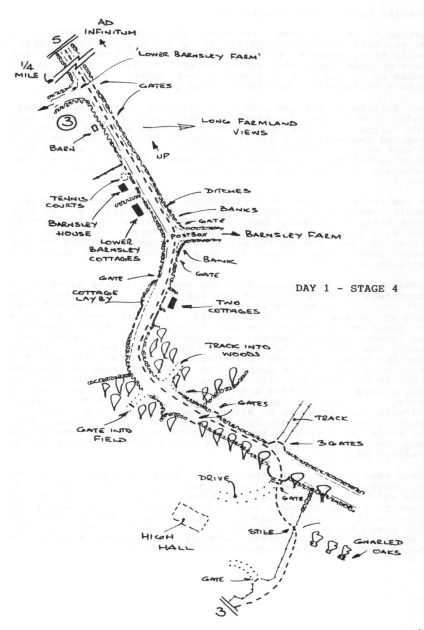

S

¼ MILE

AD INFINITUM

'LOWER BARNSLEY FARM'

GATES

LONG FARMLAND VIEWS

③

BARN

UP

TENNIS COURTS

DITCHES

BANKS

GATE

BARNSLEY HOUSE

POSTBOX

BARNSLEY FARM

LOWER BARNSLEY COTTAGES

BANK

GATE

GATE

COTTAGE LAYBY

DAY 1 - STAGE 4

TWO COTTAGES

TRACK INTO WOODS

GATES

TRACK

GATE INTO FIELD

3 GATES

DRIVE

GATE

HIGH HALL

STILE

GNARLED OAKS

GATE

3

DAY 1 - STAGE 5

Barnsley Lane to Bradford Barrow

Keeping on up this lane, counting the gates for something to
do, you will arrive eventually at a junction of farm tracks.
Before this, however, if you look carefully into the distant
trees on your left, you should be able to make out the white,
cupola up on the roof of Kingston Lacy House, one of the last
notable edifices on the final lap of Day 6.

Now, passing by the two gates at the end of the tarmac lane,
wander into an open junction area where all of the tracks have
wide verges. The first left track goes down to Chilbridge
Farm and the next left goes to Kingston Lacy. The one which
we want veers slightly right, past an open silage storage area
which is backed by a sparse hedge, past a couple of gates, and
descends, narrower and much stonier, down to another distant
junction.

In the field on your left, King Down, you can see two distinct
tumuli, the first of many on this leg of the journey - so stay
alert after the numbing haul up that tarmac lane and you'll
soon find yourself walking in the footsteps of Iron Age and
Bronze Age men, the sandal steps of the Roman invaders and the
market-bound hoof steps of many a heavy-laden Saxon and
medieval packhorse.

However, just keep going down and you will arrive at opposing
"Bridleway" signed gates astride the track. The path on the
left goes up to the tumuli whilst the path on the right just
cuts across the corner of the field to a point where it joins
our track again, around the next RH corner. After planting,
the farmer usually marks this path across the crops but,
should the route not be clear or should you feel it somewhat
churlish to march across the field when a perfectly suitable
track will lead you to exactly the same spot, keep on down the
track to the next junction and turn right. Uphill now, you
soon arrive at the track and bridleway junction by a set of
gates. Keep straight on up, past a trough in the LH field
and with distant views to Witchampton ahead of you, until the
track starts to drop slowly again, past a pair of gates across
the track, to a fork in the track. Up on the hill, behind the
hedge on your left, is the large round burial mound known as
Bradford Barrow.

Don't veer off round to the left but keep straight on, across
the verge of the shrub-filled island ahead of you , across the
lane which runs down to Old Lawn Farm, and over the farm gate
opposite you which leads into a low field. The yellow painted
arrow on the gatepost points towards the bottom RH corner of
this field and you should aim in that direction, passing under
overhead electricity cables, keeping to the hedge and close to
the electricity wires' support pole on the way.

18

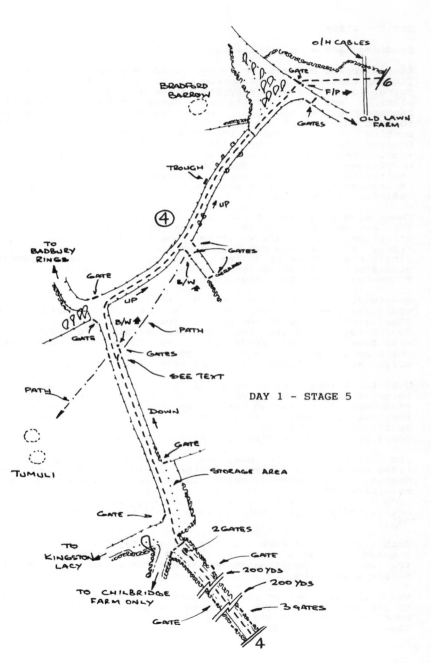

DAY 1 - STAGE 5

19

DAY 1 - STAGE 6

Bradford Barrow to Witchampton

As you approach the corner, you could have some difficulty in
finding the stile in the bottom corner of this field. The
corner is usually missed by the farmer during ploughing and/or
planting and this results in an overgrown patch, thick with
gunnera, nettles and dock. Dorset County Council have agreed
to take this matter up with the farmer concerned and the
problem may be cleared by the time you arrive in the corner.
However, on reaching the stile, a yellow arrow points up the
wide, sloping field to your left. This isn't really that
helpful on its own and doesn't ensure that you will arrive at
exactly the right spot to cross the bridged stream in the
valley on the other side of this field. So here are a few
'helpful' suggestions...

Those with a compass should aim 2 degrees East of due North.
The less well equipped should look to the far horizon in the
direction of the yellow arrow, where, amongst the skyline
trees, you will see two houses on the LH end of the trees, a
single house close by on the right of these two and several
others scattered along the skyline. The "Target" house is the
right one of the two LH end houses.

As you approach the brow of the hill, the top of a large,
round oak tree will come into view down in the valley on the
other side. When you see it, veer off slightly right from
your original "Target" route and head straight for it. This
will take you a few yards past the RH side of some wooden
posts on the top of the slope and directly down to a stiled
bridge across a tributary of the River Allen at the bottom.

Over the bridge, cross the field to a stile at the foot of the
large, round oak and, over this stile, you will find yourself
in a deep, horse-rutted but grassy hollow-way with a hedge on
the left but open, at first, on the right. Follow the track
uphill, past a bank on the left, to a junction of tracks with
newly planted woods staggered across the corners.

The next part of the hollow-way is not so straight and has
trees dotted here and there in the enclosing hedges until you
emerge, quite suddenly, onto a tarmac lane leading to a smart,
red-brick cottage on your left. Carry on down the lane, with
hedges again on both sides, to the high-banked road where a
notice informs you that the lane leads to "Malthouse Cottage
Only".

Turn right and go down the road for exactly 100 yards, passing
a gated driveway on your left, to a brick-walled garden where
the roof of a summer house peeps over the corner, underneath a
copper beech tree.

Where the signpost proclaims "Footpath. The Church", turn left
up the narrow footpath, between hedges on your left and an
assortment of walls and fences of the village cottages on your
right, until you pass a tile-topped walled garden.

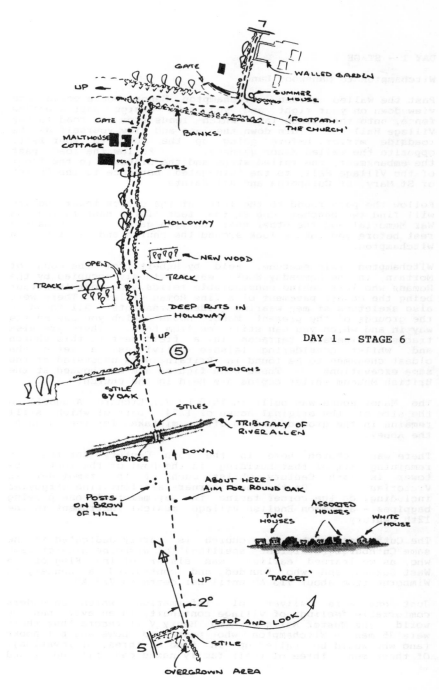

7

WALLED GARDEN

GATE

UP

SUMMER
HOUSE

GATE

'FOOTPATH.
THE CHURCH'

BANKS.

MALTHOUSE
COTTAGE

GATES

HOLLOWAY

NEW WOOD

OPEN

TRACK

TRACK

DEEP RUTS IN
HOLLOWAY

4 UP

DAY 1 – STAGE 6

⑤

TROUGHS

STILE
BY OAK

STILES

TRIBUTARY OF
RIVER ALLEN

BRIDGE

DOWN

ABOUT HERE –
AIM FOR ROUND OAK

POSTS
ON BROW
OF HILL

ASSORTED
HOUSES

TWO
HOUSES

WHITE
HOUSE

N

'TARGET'

UP

2°

STOP AND LOOK

S

STILE

OVERGROWN AREA

21

DAY 1 - STAGE 7

Witchampton to Manswood Lane

Past the walled garden, Witchampton Manor House comes into
view down on your right and you soon emerge, past a wooden
fence, onto the tarmac lane which leads from the road to the
Village Hall.   Turn down the lane and tidy yourself at the
roadside mirror before going up the road to your left,
opposite the walled Manor gardens.   Follow the road, past
the embankment, the railed steps and the driveway to the front
of the Village Hall, to the twin-gated entrance to the Church
of St Mary, St Cuthberga and All Saints.

Follow the path round to the left of the church tower and you
will find two benches, one at the foot of the bank facing the
War Memorial and the other near the lych gate.   So have a
rest before you take a look around the church and 'swot up' on
Witchampton.

Witchampton (Wichemetune, held by Hubert from the Count of
Mortain, in the Domesday Book) was previously occupied by the
Romans who left behind considerable relics, the most important
being the mosaic pavement of a fine Roman villa.   There were
also skeletons of men wearing golden ornaments - all found in
the grounds of the present Manor House which you saw on the
way in and which you can still see from here.   There are also
traces of vineyard terraces in a field next to this church
and, whilst considering leisure activities, a set of the
oldest chessmen to be found in Britain were uncovered at the
same excavations.   These bone figures are now housed at the
British Museum whilst copies are held in the church.

The Manor House was built in 1510 by Sir Richard Arundell on
the site of the original house of 1274, part of which still
remains in the grounds and is often mistaken for the ruins of
the Abbey.

There was a church here in the 13th Century but the only
remaining part of that building is the bowl of the font.   The
tower is 15th Century whilst much of the remainder is
Victorian.   On the tower corners are four fine gargoyles
including, on the corner facing the war memorial, one playing
bagpipes - a common English village musical instrument in the
12th Century.

The Cuthberga to whom the church is partly dedicated is the
same Cuthburga (different spelling) of Wimborne Minster fame
who, as we learned earlier. was sister of Ina, King of the
West Saxons, and who founded and controlled a nunnery in
Wimborne from about 713 AD until her death in 727 AD.

Just one more sliver of information which engenders
comfortable feelings of village continuity in an ever-changing
world - The Muster Rolls of King Henry VIII record that there
were 35 men in Witchampton who possessed bows and billhooks
(and who would be 'called up' in time of threat of invasion).
Of these men, three of their family names can still be found

in Witchampton.   Anyway, have a quick look around inside the church, admire the fine stained glass window,   and then you'd better get back onto the trail.

Leave the churchyard by the lych gate, over which stands a statue of St Cuthberga holding a model of Wimborne Minster, and continue up the road, past the First School on your left. Opposite the   half-timbered   house with the date '1580' emblazoned on its porch, turn left up Pound Hill, with banked hedges on either side and signposted "Manswood and Long Crichel".   But first, in commitment to our creed of spending money in every village store we find, go past Pound Hill and the bus stop to the Post Office and Store to purchase a little something - but be quick because we've already lingered a long time at the church.

Now, back at Pound Hill, passing cottages on the right and the Playing Fields on your left, you arrive at a T-junction at the top.   Turn left, signposted again to "Manswood and Long Crichel" and, opposite the solitary house, take the first lane on the right - not signposted to anywhere but known as "Sheephouse Drove".

Enjoying the downhill stroll, with wide grass verges on either side, the woods in the distance ahead are those of Chetterwood and Manswood village but you'll be turning off the road before then.   After the cantilever gate on your right which leads into Downley Coppice, past on opening on your left and a track on your right,   go under some overhead electric cables as the high banks become low once more.   Past"Sheephouse", the converted farm buildings on your left, and a Footpath post to "Rest and be Thankful 1/2" doubling back on your right, you arrive at a track with grass up the middle on your right.

Turn in along this level track, known as Rowbarrow Lane, past "Hilda Cottages" and keep straight on as the track becomes a narrower, tree and hedge-lined path with comfortable, soft grass under foot. After several bends along the way, the path emerges onto an open area with a wide, wire-fenced and blue-arrowed bridleway crossing our route.

I was startled here by a white-bellied 'golden eagle' which suddenly launched itself off the wire fence on the LH track and flapped, slowly and gracefully, into the blue sky, equally startled by my approach.   Of course, it wasn't really a golden eagle.   It was buzzard but, when you see them soaring high above your head, with their characteristic mewing call, you don't really appreciate how big they are.

Continuing up our path, with oaks reaching over your head, the first slight bend to the left gives you a first glimpse of the Ackling Dyke as it goes straight uphill after the house in the valley ahead of you.   The Roman main road to Old Sarum (the forerunner of Salisbury) from Badbury Rings and all points South and South-West will be our companion, on and off, until we arrive at the end of the first leg of our journey - at the end of Day 2 - the City of Salisbury.

I'm sorry this Stage's map is so far away from the text, but there was an awful lot of information about Witchampton - and you wouldn't have wanted to sit down in the churchyard without lots to read, would you?

St Mary, St Cuthberga and All Saints, Witchampton. Page 22

By the way, you remember I told you to pay attention because I would be asking questions later?   Well, it's now because I've got some spare space. Answers on a ten pound note to the author, please.

1. What is the name of Wimborne's restored theatre?

2. What is High Hall's oversized relation called?

3. What Farm sounds as if it should be in Yorkshire?

4. What instrument is the Witchampton gargoyle playing?

5. How long will it be before you have another sit down?

6. If you keep reading this list of questions, how long will it be before you trip in a horse shoe hole?

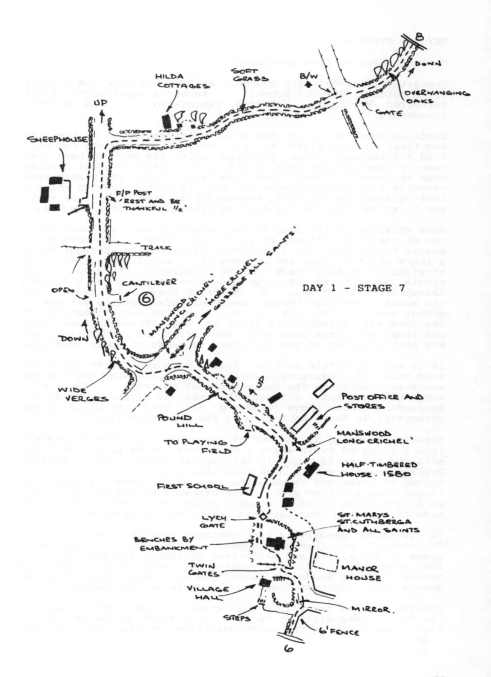

DAY 1 – STAGE 7

SOFT GRASS

HILDA COTTAGES

B/W

DOWN

OVERHANGING OAKS

GATE

UP

SHEEPHOUSE

F/P POST 'REST AND BE THANKFUL 1½'

TRACK

CANTILEVER

6

OPEN

DOWN

MORE CRICHEL. CUSBAGE ALL SAINTS

MANSWOOD LONG CRICHEL

WIDE VERGES

POST OFFICE AND STORES

POUND HILL

TO PLAYING FIELD

MANSWOOD LONG CRICHEL'

HALF·TIMBERED HOUSE. 1580

FIRST SCHOOL

LYCH GATE

ST. MARYS, ST. CUTHBERGA AND ALL SAINTS

BENCHES BY EMBANKMENT

TWIN GATES

MANOR HOUSE

VILLAGE HALL

MIRROR.

STEPS

6' FENCE

6

DAY 1 - STAGE 8

Manswood Lane to Cock Road Woods

Opposite a 'lay-by', you suddenly arrive at a gate and a fence
which borders "The Old School" - rather a magnificent, round
turretted Victorian building reminiscent of Tom Brown's
Schooldays.

Continue down the track, now with a trimmed hedge on the left
and trees on your right, to the valley bottom where you will
find a Bridleway arrow pointing back the way you have just
come, a lone pine on your right and a telephone box further
down the road. Cross over the road into the tarmac lane
opposite with Drum Cottages on the LH corner, beyond which a
turning leads to "Crichel. Manswood Play Area". At this spot,
you first set foot on the Ackling Dyke's route over the Chase.

Keep straight up the lane to an unusually long and continuous
row of thatched cottages on your left. Here, a Footpath arrow
points to the left and a Bridleway arrow points straight on up
a track which follows the RH edge of a hedged, open field. Go
straight on up this track, on the bridleway with grass up the
middle, as it turns into a wooded area of young and old mixed
hardwood and fir trees. As the track bears left, deeper into
the woods, you will become aware of wide, grassy ditches on
either side. You are walking along the actual remnants of
the Dyke and, although the track now bends through these woods
and sometimes drops down into the ditch on the RH side, you
are now following in the footsteps of ranks of Roman soldiers.

It is well to notice at this first encounter with the Roman
road that its construction ensured a dry, elevated march above
whatever conditions the route happened to cross. It is also
worth noticing that, although the road was virtually straight,
succeeding tracks have wandered all over the place whilst
attempting to maintain basically the same direction.

Anyway, arriving at the end of the woods, the Dyke disappears
into a ploughed field where a Bridleway arrow points your way
straight across to a gap in the opposite hedge. Here, another
Bridleway arrow points back into this field. Through a new
column of trees and through the gap in the hedge, go onto the
tarmac lane and turn right. The Ordnance Survey map shows the
path continuing straight ahead, across the field on the other
side of the lane, but this has long since disappeared.

In 100 yards, opposite a lone cottage, turn left onto a signed
"Bridleway" into Cock Road Woods. Follow the track, with
grass up the middle and with mixed deciduous and pine woods on
both sides, for 1/4 mile until the main track displays a
notice "Private Woods. No Entry" and our route turns off right
down a soft, narrower track which is signed "Bridleway".

Passing a grass track into the woods on the first LH bend in
the path, keep straight on down with woods on the left and a
tree-lined hedge on the right bordering the high field on your
right.

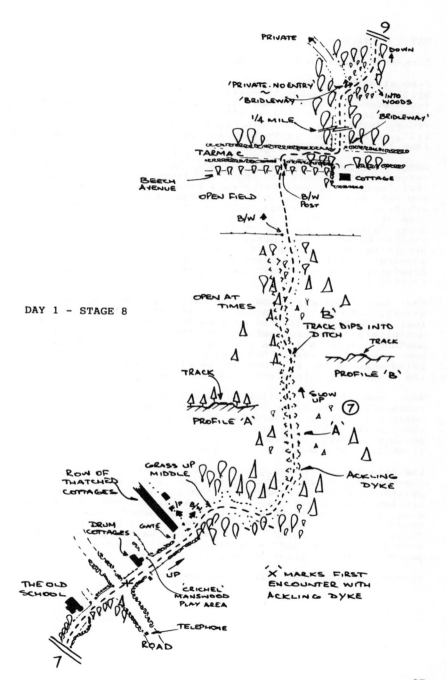

DAY 1 - STAGE 8

9

PRIVATE

DOWN

'PRIVATE. NO ENTRY'
~
'BRIDLEWAY'

INTO WOODS

'BRIDLEWAY'

1/4 MILE

TARMAC

COTTAGE

BEECH AVENUE

OPEN FIELD

B/W POST

B/W

OPEN AT TIMES

'B'

TRACK DIPS INTO DITCH

TRACK

PROFILE 'B'

TRACK

PROFILE 'A'

SLOW UP

7

'A'

ACKLING DYKE

ROW OF THATCHED COTTAGES

GRASS UP MIDDLE

DRUM COTTAGES

GATE

THE OLD SCHOOL

UP

'CRICHEL MANSWOOD' PLAY AREA

TELEPHONE

ROAD

'X' MARKS FIRST ENCOUNTER WITH ACKLING DYKE

7

DAY 1 - STAGE 9

Cock Road Woods to Sovell Down

Keep straight on down the narrow, sunken track, passing a
Bridleway arrow to the left, until you arrive, between
fence-protected new trees, at a ford and a footbridge across
Crichel stream.   Just after a stone seat (a huge block of
stone, actually) and a fingerpost pointing back to "Cock Road
1/2", a Bridleway arrow confirms your direction up the tarmac
lane slightly to your left.

Before the next bend in the road, bear off right across the
verge to a gate next to another fingerpost which proclaims
"Bridleway. Ringwood/Shaftesbury Road 1/2". Through the gate,
you are coralled between wire fences for the half mile trek
uphill to the main road.   It's only the unswerving straight
line of this uphill stretch which confirms that you are, once
more, following the line of the Ackling Dyke - no signposts or
visible banks on this acricultural section.   Anyway, arriving
breathless at the top of the field, go through the gate
adjacent to the "Bridleway. Holly Grove 1/2" signpost and very
carefully cross the busy road to the gap in the hedge slightly
to your left.

Past the Bridleway arrow, the path zig-zags somewhat whilst
trying, basically, to follow the line of the wire fence on the
left and a much overgrown embankment on your right.   This is
definitely another section of the Dyke within the dense
hawthorn scrub and, as you begin to descend, some scrub has
been cleared to reveal the Dyke more fully.   Of course, scrub
being what it is, this may not be clear when you arrive.   On
the other hand, other parts may have been cleared.

Now, passing the "Sovell Down Nature Reserve" notice, the path
veers off to the right to go around the edge of a disused
chalk pit with a protective fence which guides us along the
shady path. With the growth of trees which surround our route
on this downhill section, the Dyke itself is none to clear but
it definitely doesn't go straight down the "cliff" face.

The Dyke follows our zig-zag route down the hill and it seems
that we are now on top of it - and I had always been led to
believe that Roman roads went straight on at all times. Maybe
the Roman occupiers were human after all and couldn't scale
near-vertical hillsides in marching order any more than we
could.   This seems to be a case of "which came first - the
chalk-pit or the road?   Or was the chalk-pit dug to provide
material for the road? I've searched everywhere but can't find
enough detail to prove one way or the other.

Anyway, keep following the path downwards.

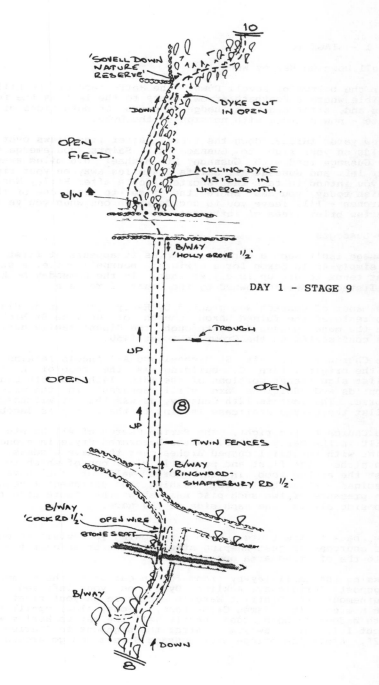

10

'SOVELL DOWN NATURE RESERVE'

DYKE OUT IN OPEN

DOWN

OPEN FIELD.

B/W ↑

ACKLING DYKE VISIBLE IN UNDERGROWTH.

B/WAY 'HOLLY GROVE 1½'

DAY 1 - STAGE 9

TROUGH

UP ↑

OPEN   OPEN

⑧

UP ↑

← TWIN FENCES

B/WAY 'RINGWOOD-SHAFTESBURY RD 1½'

B/WAY 'COCK RD 1½'   OPEN WIRE

STONE SEAT

B/WAY

↑ DOWN

⑧

DAY 1 - STAGE 10

Sovell Down to Harley Wood

Near the bottom of Sovell Down, the North face of the hill is
visible where a Footpath arrow points to the left as the fence
ends and, after a gap, a hedge appears on both sides of our
route - now a track with no sign of the Dyke.

A few yards further down the track, after fine views over the
fields on your right to Gussage All Saints, you emerge onto
the Gussage road with Gussage St Michael 0.6 miles away on
your left and Gussage All Saints 0.4 miles away on your right.
If you intend to take the shorter route after Harley Wood to
finish today, you can spare the time to visit one of these
churches - I'll leave you to decide which one when you've read
the few brief lines of introduction.

The Gussages:

Gussage isn't such a strange name as it appears at first. It
is simply Anglo-Saxon for a 'winter bourne' - i.e. a stream
that tends to dry up in dry weather. In the Domesday book, it
is listed as Gessic, owned by the Count of Mortain.

The manor of Gussage was granted by Henry I to Alan de Dinant,
who restored the ruined Saxon church of Gussage St Michael,
and the manor passed down through the Dinant family until it
was confiscated to the Crown in about 1450.

The Church to the left, St Michael and All Angels retains part
of the original 12th C. building as the base of the tower
whilst significant portions of the 13th, 14th and 15th Century
rebuilds and additions are still apparent in the existing
fabric. The font is 12th Century, as was that at Witchampton,
whilst the carved staircase leading to the belfry is Jacobean.

The Church to the right, the Parish Church of All Saints, was
built in the early 14th C. in the Decorated Style in stone and
flint with beautiful cusped arches over the nave windows. The
two niches, the first and perfectly clear one of which is just
past the arched tomb in the North wall of the nave, are
piscinas - stone basins for washing the sacramental vessels.
The presence of two such piscinas shows that there used to be
two side altars, one each side of the nave.

Now, back to the route - either following your visit to one of
the churches or just keeping straight on, cross over the road
into the off-road area opposite.

Passing the small lay-by (room for a car or two here) and the
signpost "Bridleway. Ackling Dyke" on your left and, with
Bournemouth and District Water's enclosure on your right, you
are now entering James Cross Lane, a long, slow, uphill track
with hedges on both sides nearly all the way to Harley Wood,
about 1.1/2 miles away. After the signpost to "Harley Down
1/2", cross the bridge over Gussage Stream and go around the

edge of the cantilever gate. The underfoot conditions are very pleasant now with grass up the middle of the track as you plod uphill.

Slight banks on your left and right may lead to conjecture but the one on the left is partly a remnant of the Ackling Dyke whilst the one on the right is merely the high-banked edge of the field. However, from here the Dyke becomes increasingly clear on your LH side. After two holly bushes, the track takes a right/left chicane, with the hedges ever further apart and with a green track going off at right angles on the left.

The very large barn on the right was visible as you descended Sovell Down and it is the only structure this close to the Ackling Dyke for miles. From here on, the Dyke is very clear in the hedge on your left and, where the bushes become more sparse, you can walk onto the top for short stretches.

However, after Harley Wood junction, you can walk on top of the Dyke much more easily for several miles so you may as well stay on the track for now. So keep on uphill, with grass beneath your feet and the enclosing hedges several yards apart, for another 1/4 mile.

All Saints, Gussage All Saints. Page 30

St Michael and All Angels, Gussage St Michael. Page 30

Ackling Dyke to Oakley Down. Page 36

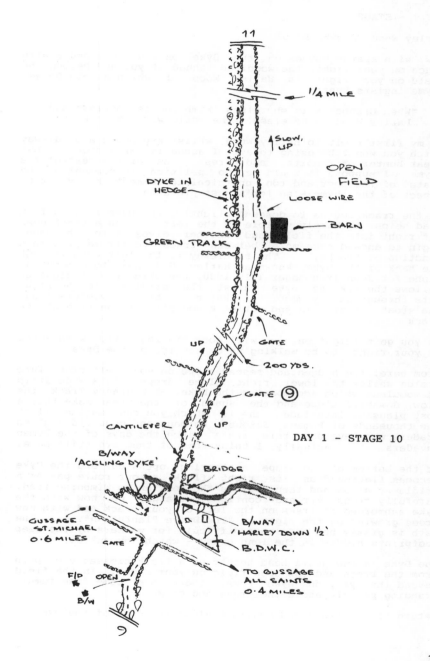

11

1/4 MILE

SLOW, UP

OPEN FIELD

DYKE IN HEDGE

LOOSE WIRE

BARN

GREEN TRACK

UP

GATE

200 YDS.

GATE ⑨

CANTILEVER

UP

DAY 1 - STAGE 10

B/WAY 'ACKLING DYKE'

BRIDGE

GUSSAGE ST. MICHAEL 0·6 MILES

GATE

B/WAY 'HARLEY DOWN 1/2'

B.D.W.C.

F/D OPEN

B/W

TO GUSSAGE ALL SAINTS 0·4 MILES

9

DAY 1 - STAGE 11

Harley Wood to Wyke Down

Now, with sparse bushes on the Dyke on your left and a wire
fence on your right, the woodland ahead of you and beyond the
field on your right is Harley Wood of which an old Dorset
rhyme insists that:

"When Cranborne is whoreless, Wimborne is poorless and
Harley Wood is hareless, the world will be at an end".

On my first visit to Harley Wood, whilst exploring a bridleway
which you won't be using today, I actually saw a stoat, that
great hunter of rabbits - and hares. As for the rest of the
rhyme, I suppose it would be too political to comment on the
state of the poor and too unethical to comment on any other
aspect of the rhyme - so let's just press on.

As the track begins to descend slightly, the Dyke reduces from
head height to barely visible on the left. As a track goes
off right into the field and another dives into the wood,
begin to ascend once more between trees to arrive at a main
junction of tracks. The bridleway to the left cuts through
the bank of the Dyke, known as Harley Gap, next to a memorial
stone for John Ironmonger 1919-1980, the bridleway straight on
follows the Ackling Dyke whilst the bridleway to the right
cuts through Harley Wood. That's the bridleway where I saw
the stoat, weaving in and out of a woodpile at the side of the
track.

As you go straight on, you will soon zig-zag left, with woods
on your right, to be walking up on the top of the Dyke.

From here, the hedged and fenced slope on your left drops into
fields whilst the lower, right slope drops into a wide strip
of woodland which accompanies the Dyke. The grassy track, the
slow, downhill slope and the shade of the trees make this a
most pleasant interlude - one in which you can imagine all of
the thousands of Romans, Saxons, Normans and good old English
Traders who have used this route since the days of the Roman
invaders. Actually, I think some of them are still here.

At the bottom of the slope, a clearing opens out and the Dyke
becomes flattened on its right flank as our route passes a
Bridleway arrow and then crosses the Monkton up Wimborne road.
Carefully cross over and continue straight on, now with the
Dyke submerged in trees on the left of your track and with new
trees growing on the right in "The Drive Plantation". The
path is grassy but made more difficult for walkers by the deep
hoofprints hidden in the long grass - watch you ankles.

The Dyke is now above head height as a track crosses your path
from the trees and the open field on your right. In the field
beyond the Dyke, on Wyke Down, there are some fine tumuli
standing proudly above the grass and crops.

Return to the track and continue along the edge of the Dyke.

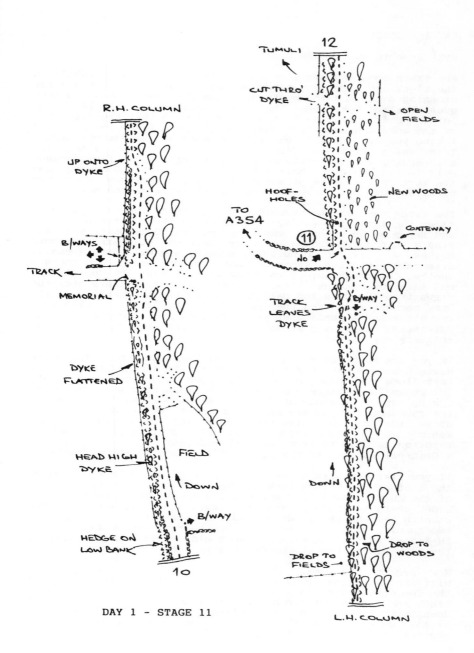

R.H. COLUMN

UP ONTO DYKE

B/WAYS

TRACK

MEMORIAL

DYKE FLATTENED

HEAD HIGH DYKE

FIELD

DOWN

B/WAY

HEDGE ON LOW BANK

10

DAY 1 - STAGE 11

TUMULI

12

CUT THRO' DYKE

OPEN FIELDS

HOOF-HOLES

NEW WOODS

TO A354

11

GATEWAY

NO

TRACK LEAVES DYKE

B/WAY

DOWN

DROP TO FIELDS

DROP TO WOODS

L.H. COLUMN

DAY 1 - STAGE 12

Wyke Down to Bottlebush Down

The track soon widens, with the woods bearing away slightly to
the right and with our path bending towards the Dyke after
crossing a track which meets us from the right and which then
goes over the Dyke into the Wyke Down tumuli field on the
left. Before bending left and right, note that the direction
of the wood's grassy track and the RH wire fence in the field
facing you are all in line with one edge of the Dorset Cursus.
This was a ceremonial route, with parallel banks almost 1/4
mile apart, which marches across Bottlebush Down from Gussage
Hill to Pentridge and Martin Down. Its exact age and purpose
are lost in the mists of antiquity and its presence is not too
clear anymore but it looks most impressive from the air.

The track now runs between the RH wire fence and the Dyke but,
after the first few yards, the grass tends to get a bit thick
and heavy so go up onto the top of the Dyke where you will
find a thin path wending its way between staggered hawthorn
bushes. If you go up early enough, you will find a small,
strangely patterned stone of indeterminate use - and there's
another, although hardly engraved at all, near the top (B3081)
end in a few minutes' time. Along the way, there are fine
views from the Dyke-top path and, after two more cuttings, the
Dyke becomes lower and then meets the B3081 with a clearing,
two gates and a small short-term pull-in for a couple of cars.
Carefully cross the road to a surprisingly positioned,
solitary apple tree.

If you are worn out now, or have already decided to leave the
Route here and get your bus or your car to finish today, turn
left along the verge to Handley Cross roundabout and lay-by
for buses to Salisbury or Blandford connections to Wimborne.
Coming from your right and riding alongside this road towards
the roundabout, you may notice an animal skin-clad, bareback
horse rider who has been seen by several motorists over many
years. His existence is treated quite seriously and is
reported as a quote from the archaeologist Dr R C C Clay by L
V Grinsell in "Dorset Barrows" 1959. See you here tomorrow!

If you like, you can divert along the B3081 to have a look at
the line of the Dorset Cursus. The wide verge on the far side
of the B3081 is usually mowed quite short and, over on that
side, there is ample parking for cars on a very long and wide
stretch between the roadside and the tree-lined fence. Before
two tumuli, one on either side of the road, an opening in the
LH fence, at the junction of two fields, gives a good view of
the edge of the Dorset Cursus in line with the woods.

Now, back to the trek. On the LH side of the apple tree, you
will find a yellow arrow-marked stile which puts you back onto
the top of the Dyke on a descending slope. There is a grassy
track and a banked field on the right and a wide, lower field
down on your left. At a cutting near the bottom of the
slope, come down off the Dyke and join the track along the
edge of the, now unfenced, RH field.

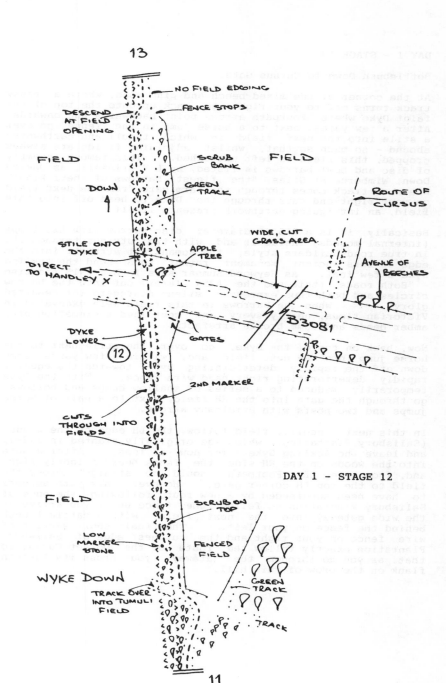

13

NO FIELD EDGING

FENCE STOPS

DESCEND AT FIELD OPENING

FIELD

FIELD

SCRUB BANK

GREEN TRACK

DOWN

ROUTE OF CURSUS

STILE ONTO DYKE

APPLE TREE

WIDE, CUT GRASS AREA

DIRECT TO HANDLEY X

AVENUE OF BEECHES

DYKE LOWER

GATES

B3081

(12)

2ND MARKER

CUTS THROUGH INTO FIELDS

DAY 1 – STAGE 12

FIELD

SCRUB ON TOP

LOW MARKER STONE

FENCED FIELD

WYKE DOWN

GREEN TRACK

TRACK OVER INTO TUMULI FIELD

TRACK

11

DAY 1 - STAGE 13

Bottlebush Down to Cursus Gate

At the corner of the mixed beech and pine wood, where a grassy track turns off to your right, go back up onto the top of the faint Dyke where Footpath arrows point backwards and onwards. After a few yards, next to a horse jump in the fence, go over a stile into the next field in which tumuli and earthworks abound - so much so that, whilst adjoining fields are always cropped, this field is left untouched. This famous assembly of disc and bowl barrows is listed, by L V Grinsell, as Oakley Down, Wimborne St Giles, "the finest barrows of their kind". Where a track comes through the farm gate from the next field on your right and cuts through the Dyke to head off into this field, an intriguing earthwork presents itself.

Basically, it is a 216 ft diameter disc barrow with two tumps (internal mounds) inside it and with two cuttings through it. In true road-builders style, the Romans cut straight into the edge of this ancient monument rather than bend the Ackling Dyke a few feet. As Heywood Sumner says in his 1913 treatise - "Both roads (this and the A354 later) cut into the barrow circles and both thus express a silent disregard for departed glory". When the barrows in this field were excavated in Victorian times, nearly every one contained a cremation urn, amber beads and some bronze artefacts.

Now, back on top of the Dyke, go over the stile next to the horse jump into the next field and, within a few yards, come down off the rapidly deteriorating Dyke towards the equally rapidly deteriorating right hand wire fence. With the Dyke temporarily reduced to a series of shallow bumps and hollows, go through the gate into the RH field, next to a pair of horse jumps and two posts with Bridleway arrows.

In this next, uphill, field follow the LH edge of the woods, (Salisbury Plantation, which was originally planted in 1939), and leave the Ackling Dyke - for now, at least. After a gate into the woods on the RH side, the fence bears slightly right and, from here, the Footpath should go straight across the field to the top LH corner gate. However, this path appears to have been superseded by a new route following the edge of Salisbury Plantation so follow the fence until you arrive at the wide gateway into the next field, with a cattle trough behind the fence on your left. The final, short section of wire fence on your right and the furthest edge of Salisbury Plantation exactly follow the route of the Dorset Cursus so that, as you go through the gateway, you cross its Eastern flank on the brow of this hill.

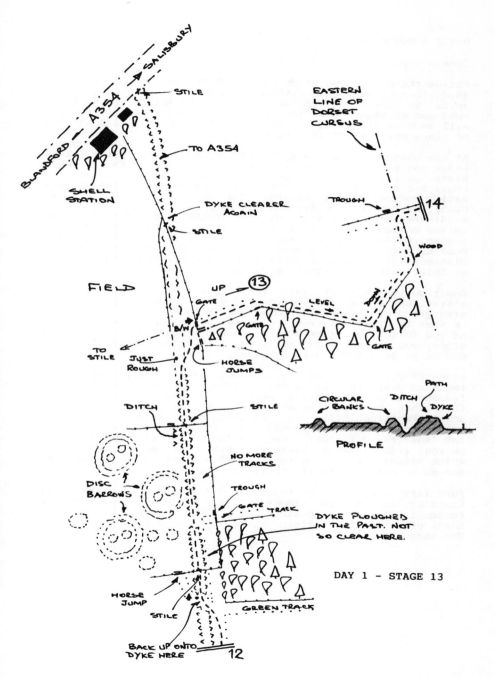

BLANDFORD — A354 — SALISBURY

STILE

TO A354

SHELL STATION

DYKE CLEARER Again

STILE

EASTERN LINE OF DORSET CURSUS

TROUGH

14

WOOD

FIELD

UP (13)

GATE

LEVEL

B/W

GATE

TO STILE

JUST ROUGH

HORSE JUMPS

GATE

DITCH

STILE

CIRCULAR BANKS

DITCH

PATH

DYKE

PROFILE

NO MORE TRACKS

TROUGH

DISC BARROWS

GATE

TRACK

DYKE PLOUGHED IN THE PAST. NOT SO CLEAR HERE.

DAY 1 — STAGE 13

HORSE JUMP

STILE

GREEN TRACK

BACK UP ONTO DYKE HERE

12

DAY 1 - STAGE 14

Cursus Gate to Pentridge Hill

Follow the descending track on the LH side of this field, with good views to Pentridge village and Church on your left. Look across to your right for views into the valley to the B3081 road and straight ahead for views of Pentridge Hill (which you will soon be ascending). Below you on your left, a long line of pines strides off into Pentridge.

At the bottom of the field, a track turns off alongside the RH hedge and your route goes past the start of that line of pines, past an opening on the left into a field and round to a boggy bit of track. This is where the Pentridge village valley bottom drains towards the headwaters of the River Crane. I hope it's dry and set hard for you. After the Bridleway arrow on a post on the right, by a gate into the valley bottom, the track bears off to the left, between hedges, to Pentridge village. Pentridge, in the Domesday Book as Pentric, was documented as belonging to the Church of Glastonbury. The name derives from the British "pen", a head or chief part and "ridge", of a hill.

Don't go that way, though. Turn right, through twin gates by a Bridleway arrow, and follow the uphill, deeply rutted track with grass up the middle, round the LH bend with an open field on your left and a narrow, wire-fenced field on your right. As you follow the sunken track, on a seemingly ever-upward slope, you go past a dug-out silage pit below you on the right and large gate posts with no gates.

With the track still deeply sunken, pass a horse jump in the fence on your right and a few scrubby bushes on both sides. Two bushes up ahead of you mark where the last gate crosses this track, next to a horse jump in the wire fence which goes across Pentridge Hill. Go through the gate onto the open grazing of the Hill where you will find tractor tracks fading into the grassy slopes. Keep following the line of the fence on your right, past a hawthorn bush, into and out off a dip which passes through the fence, past a three-barred horse jump and up to a farm gate at the top of the fence.

Turn left, away from the top right corner and follow the vague track across the upper slopes of the Hill, but keep the wire fence at the top within sight. Also, look out for grazing herds of calves and heifers - they may be nervous or playful. Who knows?

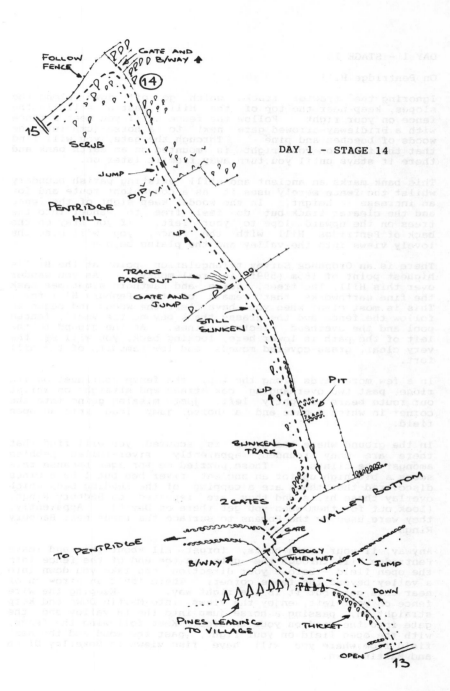

15

FOLLOW FENCE

GATE AND B/WAY

(14)

SCRUB

JUMP

DIP

PENTRIDGE HILL

UP

TRACKS FADE OUT

GATE AND JUMP

STILL SUNKEN

PIT

UP

SUNKEN TRACK

2 GATES

VALLEY BOTTOM

GATE

TO PENTRIDGE

B/WAY

BOGGY WHEN WET

JUMP

DOWN

PINES LEADING TO VILLAGE

THICKET

OPEN

13

DAY 1 - STAGE 15

On Pentridge Hill

Ignoring the tractor tracks which go off down along the slopes, keep near the top of the Hill, past a stile in the fence on your right. Follow the fence until you meet a fence with a Bridleway-arrowed gate next to a horse-jump into the woods of beeches and pine   Through the gate, you will find that the fence on your right is mounted on an earth bank and there it stays until you turn away from it later on.

This bank marks an ancient and still existing parish boundary whilst the fence merely uses it as a convenient route and for an increase in height. In the woods, keep sight of the fence and the clearer track but do feel free to wander into the trees on the upward slope to your left. If you stay on the back of Pentridge Hill with the fence, you will miss the lovely views into the valley and the plains beyond.

There is an Ordnance Survey triangulation point at the Hill's highest point of 185m (599ft in real money). As you wander over this Hill, the trees, gorse and hawthorn sometimes mask the fine earthworks that remain of the Penbury Hill fort. This is most clear when you have left the woods and begun to follow the fence and the grassy track beyond the small, fenced pool and the overhead electric lines. As the ground to the left of the path is lower here, looking back, you will see the very clear, grass-covered mounds and low ramparts of the hill fort.

In a few more yards along the top, the fence continues on its ridge, past two overhanging oak trees and straight on whilst our route bears slightly left, just missing going into the corner in which a gate and a horse jump lead into an open field.

In the ground where the grass is scoured, you will find that there are many rounded, apparently river-rolled pebbles amongst the flints. These puzzled me for ages because this seems a bit high up for an ancient river bed but I have since discovered that these are a capping of the Reading beds which overlay these hills and they are repeated on Badbury Rings. (Look out for them when you get there on Day 6). Apparently, they were used by the Romans to surface the roads near Badbury Rings.

Anyway, if your brain hurts, forget all about this and leave Pentridge Hill through the gate in the end of the fence into the open field - before your direction can take you down into a valley beyond the fence corner. There isn't an arrow on or near this gate but it IS the right way. Keeping the wire fence on your left, enjoy the views into Martin Down and keep straight on, passing a horse jump into the LH valley and the gate into the wood on your LH side. Keep following the fence, with the open field on your right, past the wood and the next field from where you will have fine views to Bokerley Ditch and Martin Down.

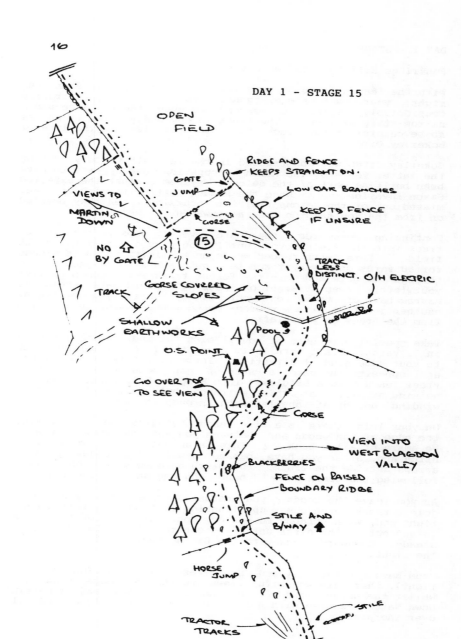

16

DAY 1 - STAGE 15

OPEN FIELD

RIDGE AND FENCE KEEPS STRAIGHT ON.

LOW OAK BRANCHES

GATE JUMP

KEEP TO FENCE IF UNSURE

VIEWS TO MARTIN DOWN

GORSE

⑮

NO BY GATE

TRACK LESS DISTINCT. O/H ELECTRIC

TRACK

GORSE COVERED SLOPES

SHALLOW EARTHWORKS

POOL

O.S. POINT

GO OVER TOP TO SEE VIEW

GORSE

VIEW INTO WEST BLAGDON VALLEY

BLACKBERRIES

FENCE ON RAISED BOUNDARY RIDGE

STILE AND B/WAY

HORSE JUMP

STILE

TRACTOR TRACKS

14

43

DAY 1 - STAGE 16

Pentridge Hill to Bokerley Ditch

With the fenced field on your left and the open field on your right, your path slopes gently downwards and, narrowing considerably, begins to descend between the LH fence and a narrow strip of trees. The track is now badly holed by horses so be careful as you look down on your left to the line of Bokerley Ditch.

Bokerley Ditch was constructed in the late 4th Century during the latter years of the Roman occupation and appears to have been built as part of the defence system against the expected Saxon invasion. When the Romans left Britain, Dorset was missed out of the Saxons' initial incursion, when they pressed on from the Southampton area northwards.

Continuing downwards, there are several gaps in the line of trees into the field beyond until you pass a gate into the LH field. Here, with fenced woods on the left, the path widens for 50 yards on its approach to a gate and a horse jump. Go through the gate and join the forest track which comes up from your left. Keep straight on, passing a field gate beyond the narrow band of trees on your right, until you arrive at another junction with a wooden-fenced track coming to meet you from the trees on your left.

Take special care here or you'll miss the indistinct bridleway in 50 yards. Don't turn left down the forest track but keep to your same general direction. There is a gate on your right and, opposite the gate, a step-up gap between the trackside trees leads onto a bridleway into Blagdon Hill Wood. There is no sign or arrow at this entrance but follow the narrow, winding, hoofprint-labelled path through the woods.

On your left, there is a wire fence bounding the field beyond the edge of the woods and, between you and the fence, you will be aware of a low bank. This is an outer flank of Bokerley Ditch and, after you have passed a pair of Bridleway painted arrows astride the track, the Ditch becomes more clear until, following the track on a LH bend, you emerge into the light.

As you leave the woods, you instantly cross Bokerley Ditch to join a track which comes up alongside it from your left. Bear right and, with scrubby bushes on your left, follow the track in and out of the ditch until it eventually settles down to a steady, downward track with the Ditch bearing off slowly to the right.

From here, in Easterly and South-Easterly directions (front right), there are wonderful views to the very edge of England whilst the scrub opens out to the clearer downland of Martin Down Nature Reserve with dozens of chalk molehills dotted all over the place.

44

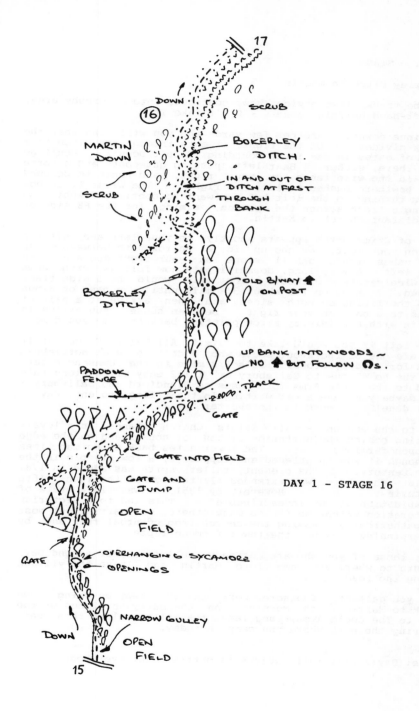

17

DOWN

(16)

SCRUB

MARTIN
DOWN

BOKERLEY
DITCH.

IN AND OUT OF
DITCH AT FIRST
THROUGH
BANK

SCRUB

TRACK

BOKERLEY
DITCH

OLD B/WAY ↑
ON POST

UP BANK INTO WOODS ~
NO ↑ BUT FOLLOW Ωs.

PADDOCK
FENCE

WOOD TRACK

GATE

GATE INTO FIELD

TRACK

GATE AND
JUMP

DAY 1 - STAGE 16

OPEN
FIELD

GATE

OVERHANGING SYCAMORE

OPENINGS

NARROW GULLEY

DOWN

OPEN
FIELD

15

DAY 1 - STAGE 17

Bokerley Ditch to Martin

As the track, less obvious now, continues into a scrubby area,
a left-hand hairpin appears - Don't take it!

Continue down for another few yards and you will find that the
track divides.   On the right, it cuts through the Ditch to a
pair of gates in the fence bounding "Tidpit Down".   Don't go
down there, either.   Bear left, passing gateposts and a horse
jump in the wire fence on your right, and begin to descend
with hawthorn bushes to left and right.   The wider track now
keeps turning to the left but you want to continue downhill on
a single track across the common, aiming for the RH side of
the distant church in Martin.

Part of Grims Ditch appears shortly on your left and, after a
pit on your left, you end up in a narrow path between trees
and bushes with an uphill slope on your right and a drop on
your left.   A very long, downhill path now follows, with dense
and wide verges, without which this would be a wide track
indeed.   Keep on for about 3/4 mile until you pass openings
into the fields on both sides and then arrive at a pair of
gates to a barn on your right.   Between houses, you arrive in
Martin with a Bridleway arrow pointing back the way you came.

Turn left if you would like to visit All Saints Church or if
you are one of the stout souls who didn't leave at Bottlebush
Down for Handley Cross.   It's 1/2 mile to the Townsend estate
for the No 42 bus to Salisbury or 1.1/2 easy miles along this
road to the Coote Arms for buses to Blandford and Salisbury -
or maybe you have a car waiting in the village to end Day 1.
Well done!   Yours is the shorter Day 2.

Now to the church - All Saints Church stands in a lovely
setting behind the Northside ribbon of houses and on the edge
of open farmland.   The tower dates back to Norman times
although it was heightened and topped by a low steeple in the
15th Century.   The present, taller, spire was added in 1787
whilst the church was extended all throughout the 13th - 16th
Centuries.   However, by 1851, it was "in a state of
dilapidation almost indescribable".   This led to a Victorian
restoration which, unlike so many others, was carried out most
sympathetically, saving the church from eventual ruin and, by
underpinning, saving the tower from collapse.

Now, those of you who are already well into your second Day,
return to where you came into Martin and leave the village
along the road.

For you gallant, footsore warriors who kept on going, come
back to Martin in the morning, on the early No 42 bus or the
184 to The Coote Arms, and leave the village along this road,
passing the path where you came in today.

Note: Day 2 officially starts in Martin - for everybody.

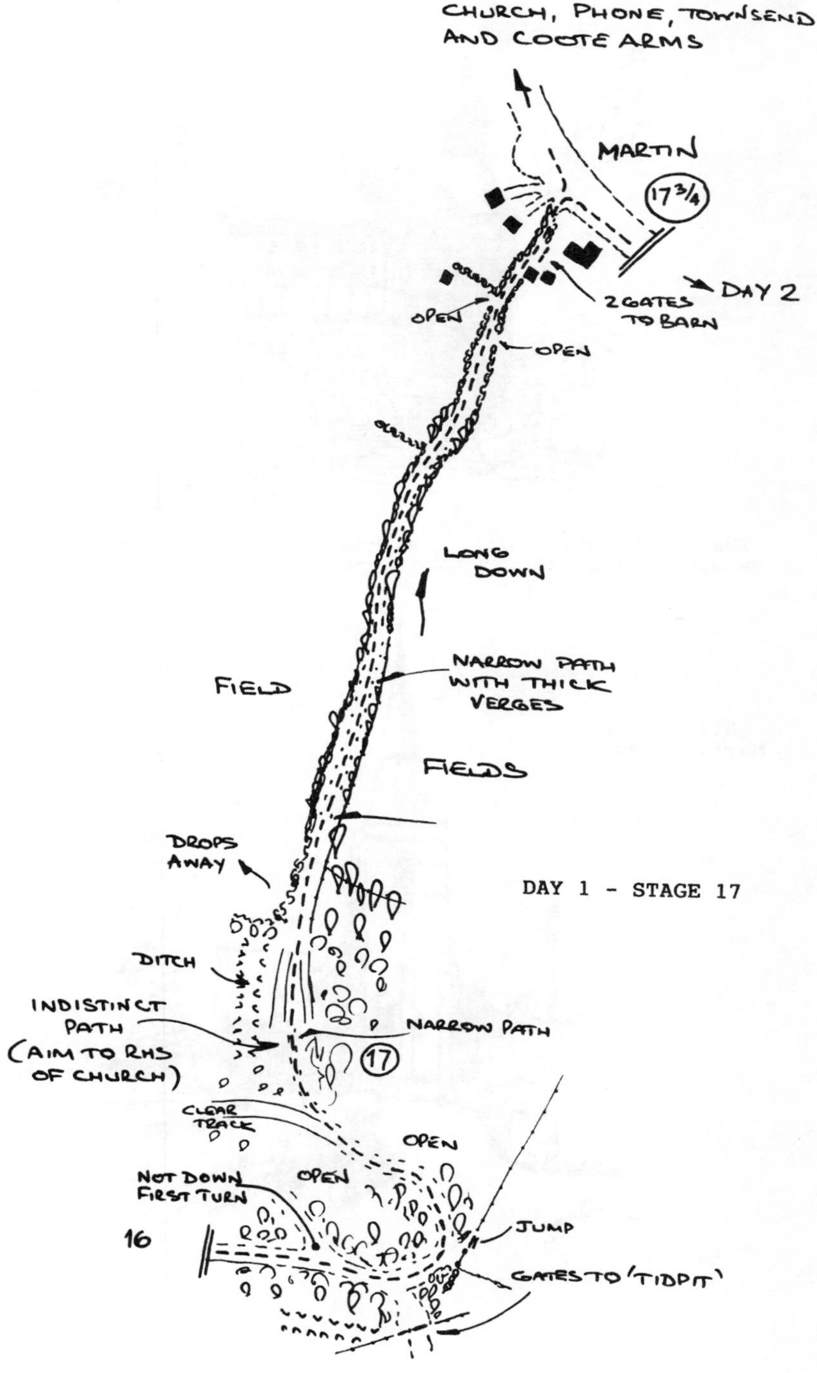

CHURCH, PHONE, TOWNSEND
AND COOTE ARMS

MARTIN

17¾

DAY 2

2 GATES
TO BARN

OPEN

OPEN

LONG
DOWN

NARROW PATH
WITH THICK
VERGES

FIELD

FIELDS

DROPS
AWAY

DAY 1 - STAGE 17

DITCH

INDISTINCT
PATH
(AIM TO RHS
OF CHURCH)

NARROW PATH

17

CLEAR
TRACK

OPEN

NOT DOWN
FIRST TURN

OPEN

16

JUMP

GATES TO 'TIDPIT'

47

The Old School,
Manswood. Page 26

All Saints,
Martin. Page 46

DAY 2 INTRODUCTION

Martin to Salisbury

The remnants of the old Weymouth and Poole road to Salisbury begin Day 2, taking you over Toyd Down, through agricultural land and sheep grazing pastures into South Wiltshire where you soon find the lovely, tranquil village of Stratford Tony with its tiny church. You walk straight across the race track of the historic Salisbury Racecourse which stands on top of the downs, parallel to the old Drovers' Road between Shaftesbury and Salisbury with the Ebble river valley on this side and the Nadder river valley on the other.

Another easy stroll along the Ackling Dyke, just beyond this Racecourse, brings you to the water meadows and along the Town Path from where John Constable painted the view of the Cathedral made famous through millions of prints, table mats and drinks coasters which bear images of this masterpiece.

From there, it is a matter of moments before your arrival into the heart of Salisbury and Day's end in the Close of this most magnificent of Cathedrals. And, if you start today early enough, you can take an gentle stroll around the city of Salisbury, call in at the Cathedral or visit Mompesson House, in the Close.

You only need O S Map No 184 so there's less to carry today.

	STAGE	MILES	TOTAL
1	Martin to Toyd Down	1.25	1.25
2	Toyd Down to Little Toyd Down	1.25	2.50
3	Little Toyd Down to Stratford Tony	1.75	4.25
4	Stratford Tony to Ackling Dyke	2	6.25
5	Ackling Dyke to Salisbury Racecourse	1.25	7.50
6	Salisbury Racecourse to Water Meadows	1.50	9
7	Water Meadows to Town Path	1	10
8	Town Path to Salisbury Cathedral	1	11

Altogether a much easier day than Day 1 but, nonetheless, it follows ancient routes over high ground with fine views, low meadowland with tranquil streams and wide water meadows with formerly navigable rivers. You have the chance to visit a particularly restful, stone and flint church and to, legally, get onto a racecourse without paying.

If you kept going to the end on Day 1, you only have 11 miles to do today, so take it easy and enjoy all of the stops.

DAY 2 - STAGE 1

Martin to Toyd Down

Arriving in Martin on the early No 42 bus, the later 184 to
The Coote Arms or by personal transport, walk past the narrow
Bridleway where you arrived in Martin at the end of Official
Day 1 and, after the stream crosses the road from left to
right, go past a Footpath sign on the left. Shortly, after a
thatched cottage on the corner of the lane to East Martin, a
grassy common on the far corner and a small parking area on
your right, you will arrive at a bridge across the road under
which a deep ditch runs from left to right. Immediately after
the bridge, turn off the road by the Hampshire County
Council's "Footpath" sign on the LH side.

In the narrow, grassy and sunken path, with trees on the left
and a banked hedge on the right, keep on until the ditch runs
out by a yellow-banded tree. Just after this marker, turn up
the bank into the field on your right by the double "Footpath"
arrows and a yellow post. Stepping up into the high field,
you will see Windmill Hill directly ahead of you and, as you
follow the RH hedge across this field, there are fine views
back to Martin. Passing an opening in the hedge and two
holly trees, you emerge through the facing hedge onto a tarmac
drive with yet another Footpath sign.

Turn left here onto the uphill lane which is a remnant of the
old main road from Poole and Weymouth to Salisbury which used
to pass through Cranborne before the construction of the Great
Western Turnpike, begun in 1755.

With the banked hedge around the foot of Windmill Hill on your
right and open views across the unfenced field on your left,
ignore the Footpath sign on your right by two farm gates but
keep straight on, now onto a concrete stretch which passes a
large barn on your right. The concrete finishes by a wooden
fence with a farm gate on your right which leads to a farm and
its outbuildings. Then, with a chalk and clay track beneath
your feet, you have a field hedge on your left and a trimmed
leylandii hedge on your right until, after another gate, the
hedge gives way to a continuous wire fence. Dropping now,
with barrows visible on the right skyline, the track begins to
descend, passing more gates on either side, to a watersplash
at the bottom of the dip. The very wide track has enabled a
grassy by-pass to develop but, as this splash is always there,
it would seem a simple matter to dig a ditch between it and
the field below it and let the water run away into the steeply
dropping field.

Anyway, start to ascend now, with some bushes on the right and
still with a hedge on the left, and ignore the turn off to the
right and the track which runs up onto the spit of high ground
between that route and the main track. Keep on past more
gates and with the verge varying in depth to right and left.

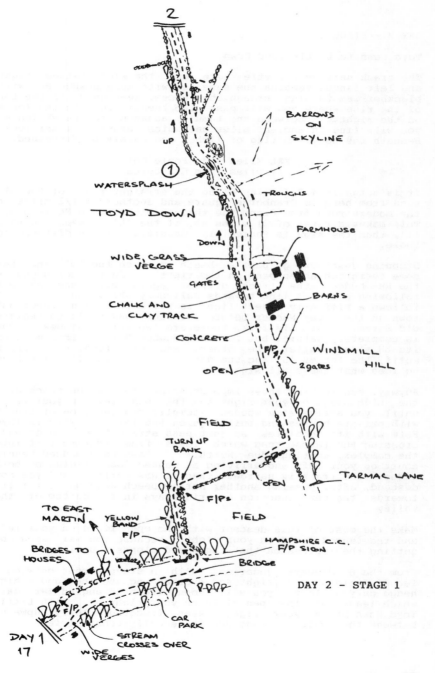

2

BARROWS
ON
SKYLINE

UP

WATERSPLASH ①

TROUGHS

TOYD DOWN

FARMHOUSE

DOWN

WIDE, GRASS
VERGE

GATES

BARNS

CHALK AND
CLAY TRACK

CONCRETE

F/P

WINDMILL
HILL

OPEN

2 gates

FIELD

TURN UP
BANK

TARMAC LANE

OPEN

TO EAST
MARTIN

F/Ps

YELLOW
BAND

F/P

FIELD

BRIDGES TO
HOUSES

HAMPSHIRE C.C.
F/P SIGN

BRIDGE

DAY 2 - STAGE 1

F/P

CAR
PARK

DAY 1
17

STREAM
CROSSES OVER

WIDE
VERGES

51

DAY 2 - STAGE 2

Toyd Down to Little Toyd Down

The track narrows a little here but the width between right
and left fences remains the same so, with more bushes and with
blackberries twining through the fences, keep on up to the top
of the rise where you will pass two tumuli close to the fence
on the right. Between the tumuli, adjacent to the RH fence,
you will find an ancient milestone which repays a closer look.
Beneath the heavy coating of lichen can barely be discerned:

XXL Miles from Poole Gate
IV Miles from Cranborne

It is actually 4.3/4 miles along the straight route of the old
road from here to Cranborne Square and another 16.1/2 miles on
the modern road from Cranborne through Wimborne to Poole Quay.
This makes a total of 21 miles so, if the 'L' is meant to be a
'I', then the sign is incredibly accurate for the distance to
Poole.

Dropping down now, go past a beech wood on the left and then
some overgrown sheep pens on the right. Just after a gap in
the RH hedge, the track divides again with the RH fork
following a direct line towards Salisbury whilst our, LH, fork
follows a similarly direct line to Wilton, the most important
town on the River Nadder before Salisbury was built to replace
Old Sarum. At this fork, there are two marker stones. One
is completely natural but for an Ordnance Survey bench mark on
its LH side, whilst the other, smaller stone, has a crown
motif, the letter 'S' and the date '1891' - but I really have
no idea what these all signify.

Anyway, considering these imponderables, follow the track with
the high hedge on your right and the open field on your left,
until you arrive at a wooded, complicated junction of tracks
with private houses and buildings on the left. This is Toyd
Farm with its accolytes so just pass straight on through and,
crossing the tarmac road which leads from right to left into
the complex, continue due North. Passing a hedged tennis
court on your left and arriving at banked, open fields on both
sides, the track is narrower than it was earlier and you now
descend, after passing another narrow beech wood on your left,
towards the next junction of Bridleways in the bottom of the
valley.

Make the most of this descent with the open field on your left
and the fenced field on your right, because you will soon be
getting the impression that the world slopes - uphill.

From the Bridleways' junction, with a steep ascent between a
fenced field on your right and overhanging beeches and a high
hedge on your left, you will soon reach an angled farm gate
which leads into the open field on your right. With Little
Toyd Down up on your right, keep trudging slowly upwards
between the constant hedge and the equally constant fence.

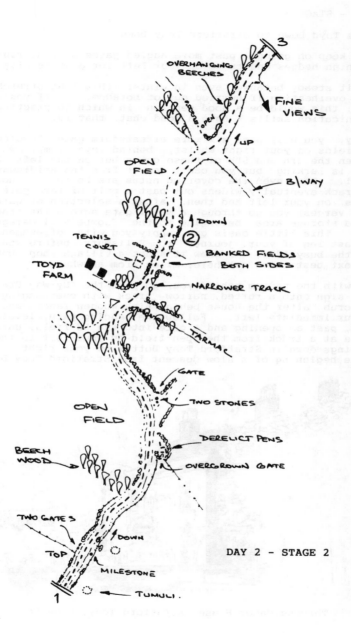

OVERHANGING
BEECHES

3

FINE
VIEWS

OPEN

UP

OPEN
FIELD

B/WAY

DOWN

2

TENNIS
COURT

BANKED FIELDS
BOTH SIDES

TOYD
FARM

NARROWER TRACK

TARMAC

GATE

OPEN
FIELD

TWO STONES

DERELICT PENS

BEECH
WOOD

OVERGROWN GATE

TWO GATES

TOP

DOWN

DAY 2 - STAGE 2

MILESTONE

1

TUMULI.

DAY 2 - STAGE 3

Little Toyd Down to Stratford Tony Down

Just keep on going, past more angled gates on your right and more high hedges and trees on your left for a whole mile.

Take it steady because, even in winter, this long stretch will cause overheating if hurried out of boredom. If you're not alone, this would be a good section in which to practice your communication skills - have a good chat, that is.

Anyway, you will pass six more offset farm gates leading into the fields on your right whilst, behind Toyd Clump, which is between the 4th and 5th of these gates but on the left, Grim's Ditch is lurking but you can't see it from the Bridleway, if at all. See, even the covering notes are boring. However, the track eventually widens out past a pair of farm gates into fields on your left and then, after a selection of gates and grass verges, you go through a metal gate across the track and into a storage area belonging to the "Coombe Hill Garage" and Shop. This little oasis can supply you with refreshments for the last leg of your journey to Salisbury before you cross over the busy A354. I know it's not a village shop, but it's the next best thing out here, miles from anywhere.

Now, with the tedium behind you, go past the "By-Way Stratford Tony" sign onto a rutted, narrow track with overhanging trees and scrub after the house behind high wooden fences and gates on your immediate left. Follow the bending path, level for a while, past an opening and a gate into the LH field, until you arrive at a track from the open field on your left to the farm buildings down in Stratford Tony Bottom on your right. This is the beginning of a slow descent from Stratford Tony Down.

Throope Manor House, Stratford Tony. Page 56

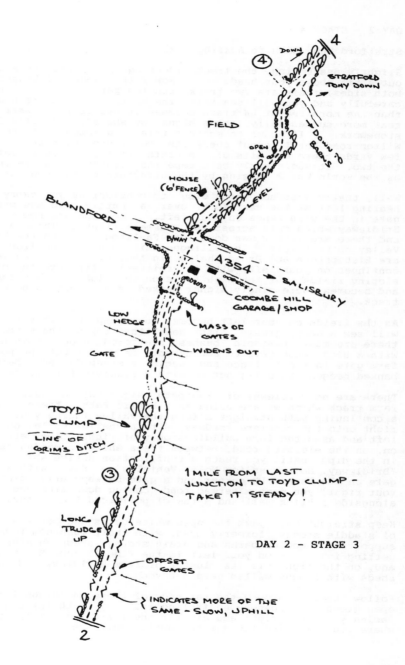

DOWN

④

4

STRATFORD
TONY DOWN

FIELD

DOWN TO
BARNS

OPEN?

HOUSE
(6' FENCE)

LEVEL

BLANDFORD

B/WAY

A354 ➔ SALISBURY

COOMBE HILL
GARAGE/SHOP

LOW
HEDGE

MASS OF
GATES

GATE

WIDENS OUT

TOYD
CLUMP

LINE OF
GRIM'S DITCH

③

1 MILE FROM LAST
JUNCTION TO TOYD CLUMP –
TAKE IT STEADY!

LONG
TRUDGE
UP

DAY 2 – STAGE 3

OFFSET
GATES

⟩ INDICATES MORE OF THE
SAME – SLOW, UPHILL

2

DAY 2 - STAGE 4

Stratford Tony Down to Ackling Dyke

Slightly descending, the track widens again and the trees thin
out a bit above your head.   Now with bushes and hedges on
both sides, there are two tracks running parallel.   Look
carefully and you will see that the RH track, which is higher
than the more recent LH track because it has resisted wear and
tear more successfully, shows signs of shaped, carefully laid
stonework.   It seems to me that this is a remnant of the old
Wilton road but I cannot guess its age or who built it.   In a
few yards there are bits of concrete in it, so don't confuse
the two.   It has clearly been repaired frequently, as recently
as the World War 2 judging by the structure of the concrete.

Well, that's just something else to consider as you carry on,
bearing left at the next fork over a cattle grid and past a
gate in the wire fence on your left.   You are now on the
Bridleway which cuts across the Western flank of Throope Hill
and there are fine views down into Faulston Down and the Ebble
Valley on your left.   The villages which you can see from here
are Bishopstone and Broad Chalke, in that order.   The fence
continues on your left, with intermittent gates into the steep
sloping fields, but the high field on the right stays unfenced
and becomes increasingly higher banked as you keep on down the
track.

As the fields on your left become too steep to cultivate, you
will see a deep, grassy dish near the top of the slope and
there are many hawthorn bushes scattered around this area.
With a high, bush covered embankment on your right, go past a
farm gate in the LH fence and begin a steep descent, between
banked hedges, to a T-junction with a concrete farm track.

There are no Bridleway or Footpath signs but, as well as the
farm track which we are using as a Public Path, there is also
a continuing path straight across the valley facing you.   Turn
right onto the concrete roadway, with a shallow valley on your
left and assorted farm buildings on your right. Keep straight
on, on the elevated road, between trees and with wooden fences
in the dips, until you reach a confirmation notice which reads
"Bridleway. No Access for Motor Vehicles".   Here, with a farm
gate on the banked LH corner and a gate between brick piers on
your right, you meet a tarmac road coming down from your left
alongside a brick wall and a row of pollarded lime trees.

Keep straight on, past the open white gates and between rows
of staddle stones (formerly used, with their mushroom tops, as
supports for wooden barns and grain storage sheds to stop rats
getting in).   On your left is the fine Throope Manor House
and, on the right, is its cluster of farm buildings and wooden
sheds with a huge walled garden beyond.

Follow the road around the far end of these buildings into an
open green with roadway encircling it.   With three houses
facing you, turn right and aim for the far corner of the green
where you will find the narrow, uphill entrance to a shady and

hedge lined hollow-way which leads to Stratford Tony Church of
St Mary and St Lawrence. In case of difficulty, the path runs
alongside the hedge of the farthest cottage on the green.
Continuing up the hollow-way, with hedges on both sides, go
past a small personnel gate on your left and, as the path gets
narrower and levels out, go past the angled farm gate which
leads into the field also on your left.   Immediately, the
hedge runs out and a wire fence begins and, across the fence,
you will see the lovely Church of Stratford Tony nestling on
the downward slopes behind an assortment of trees and bushes.

Don't bother going over the stiles on either side of the small
field as it's just as easy to go round the edge.   So keep
straight on, with the field on your left and the hedge on your
right, to the track which emerges from between the trees on
your right.   Turn sharp left here and, passing several wooden
garages on your right, follow the track until a side, grassy
path goes down to the right by the church.   Take this track
and, in the bank on your left you will find the entrance gate
to the churchyard.   Through the gate, turn right and go round
to the back of the church where you will find the entrance in
the side porch.

Stratford Tony derives its name from two sources.   The first
part confirms that it was here that the Ackling Dyke crossed
the River Ebble by a ford.   Strat = Street, Ford = Ford.   The
second part, Tony, comes from Ralph de Toni, William the
Conqueror's standard bearer at the battle of Hastings, to whom
the manor of Stratford was given as a reward.

It is possible that this church structure stands on the
foundations of its 13th Century predecessor.   The chancel is
14th Century flint with stone dressings whilst the tower arch
and porch are about 1500.   The font and piscina are most
likely remnants of the 13th Century original.   The remaining
major areas date from between 1630 and mid 18th Century whilst
much of the internal arrangement, including pews, chancel
stalls and pulpit are all pre-17th Century.

The church is well worth an exploration and it would welcome
your donation especially as it is now maintained solely by the
Redundant Churches Fund.

Now, leaving the church, carry on down the grassy track to the
steel and concrete footbridge which crosses the River Ebble
just after some cottages on this side.   Just outside Cawden
Cottage is a lovely bench where you can rest your weary limbs
and thank Jennifer Shepherd to whom this bench is dedicated.

This is a beautiful and peaceful spot where "still glides the
stream", although the ducks are usually, noisily arguing just
upstream.   Make the most of this as, I'm sure you will have
realized, you are in a valley at the moment so you have to go
uphill again to approach our goal city of Salisbury.   So,
raise yourself once more and carry on along the tarmac
footpath around the far end of Cawden Cottage.   Crossing a
ditch by the small bridge, follow the low, tile topped wall to
join the tarmac lane ahead, whilst ignoring the two branches

of the lane that go off on your right.

Now the wall is higher and there is a stream running along the RH side of the lane. After a gate into the field on the right, you arrive at a brick-walled bridge under which a small stream flows and immediately after the bridge, a large pair of wooden gates down on your left still bear the peeling painted name of "Poole Foundry" - an organization which disappeared in the late 1970's. After another gate in the hedge on your right, and following the pine hedge on your left, the house on the right has a fine, high flint and render garden wall facing Manor Farm and its buildings over on your left.

Immediately after these, you arrive at a road junction with a grass verge and a post box on the near RH corner. On the LH corner is a signpost for "Wilton" straight on (our way), for Shaftesbury to the left and for Salisbury to the right. Cross over the road into the banked and hedged road opposite, being careful of approaching traffic from both directions. In 100 yards, there is a rough lay-by on the right and, just a few yards past this, the line of the Bridleway which goes off to your right is a continuation of the line of the road emerging from your left. Once more, this is the route of the Ackling Dyke and you rejoin it as it turns up the stony track, between hedges, on the right.

St Mary and St Lawrence, Stratford Tony. Page 57

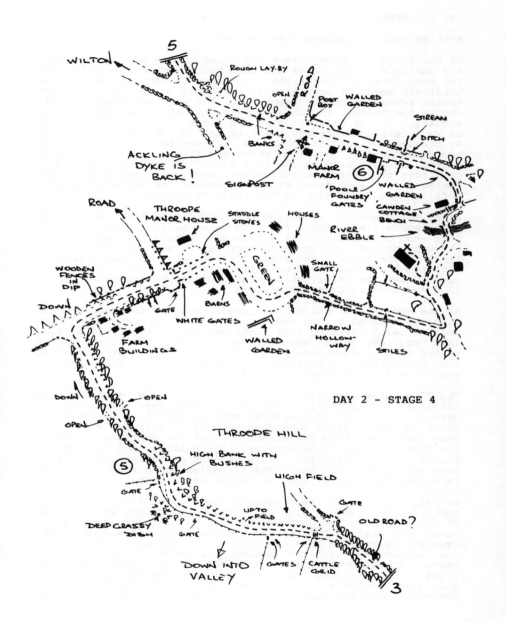

5

WILTON

ROUGH LAY.BY

OPEN

POST BOX

WALLED GARDEN

STREAM

DITCH

BANKS

ACKLING DYKE IS BACK!

SIGNPOST

MANOR FARM

'POOLE FOUNDRY' GATES

WALLED GARDEN

CAWDEN COTTAGE BEECH

(6)

ROAD

THROOPE MANOR HOUSE

STADDLE STONES

HOUSES

RIVER EBBLE

WOODEN FENCES IN DIP

GREEN

DOWN

GATE

WHITE GATES

BARNS

SMALL GATE

FARM BUILDINGS

WALLED GARDEN

NARROW HOLLOW-WAY

STILES

DOWN

OPEN

OPEN

DAY 2 - STAGE 4

THROODE HILL

(5)

HIGH BANK WITH BUSHES

HIGH FIELD

GATE

UP TO FIELD

OLD ROAD?

GATE

DEEP GRASSY DISH

GATE

DOWN INTO VALLEY

GATES

CATTLE GRID

3

DAY 2 - STAGE 5

Ackling Dyke to Salisbury Racecourse

Up the rough and stony track, go round the LH side of the gate
and continue, past barns and farm buildings on your left and
the open field on your right, to the much narrower section of
bridleway ahead of you, with a high hedge on the left and some
sparse sycamores on the right. The path now descends and,
whilst the hedges are further apart, it stays very narrow and
winding. At the bottom of the slope, there is a pine wood
on your left and, through the farm gate across your path, the
Bridleway continues to be narrow but now follows the RH hedge
of an open field, uphill on chalk and flint. The field
begins to fall away on the left and, just before you reach a
gate into the field on your right where the more-used track
emerges, you get a first glimpse, beyond the woods up on your
left, of the Grandstand at Salisbury Racecourse.

Still going uphill, alongside the hedge and fence on your RH
side, you arrive, with a few pine trees on your right and near
to a wood on your left, at a farm gate across your path. Go
through the gate and cross another farm track onto the greener
track on the other side, still straight on. The fields on
both sides are now level whilst, across the one on the right,
you can see the interlocking spurs of the valley in which the
A354 descends to Coombe Bissett.

At the end of your field, you reach another farm gate in the
wire fence which brings you onto a tarmac lane where you turn
left. With scrub on your right and the fenced field on your
left, you come to a wooded area through which you meet a
rutted track across your path. This is the Old Drovers' Road
from Shaftesbury to Salisbury - more of which later when you
start Day 3 along this very road.

The Racecourse was laid out up here, high on the downs outside
Salisbury and parallel to the old Drovers' Road, because Henry
Herbert, 2nd Earl of Pembroke and incumbent of Wilton House
which is just 2 miles away down the hill, initiated a 14 miles
long horse race from Whitesheet Hill at the Shaftesbury end of
the Drovers' Road to Harnham at the Salisbury end towards the
end of the 16th Century. This was not an annual event but it
drew vast crowds and additional, regular races resulted in the
later construction of this permanent Racecourse.

Anyway, duck under the plastic rails, after making sure that
there isn't a race in progress, and cross to the smart course
of the Salisbury and South Wilts Golf Club. This course is
built with Ackling Dyke as its Eastern boundary and your route
exactly follows its line downhill to the Nadder Valley. Now,
cut across the first tee behind the hedge leading onto the
course, go round the back of the next tee and immediately turn
right. Follow this line past the back of the 15th tee,
turn left and you will find the entrance to the Dyke route,
between hedges and many fine beech trees on the downward path.

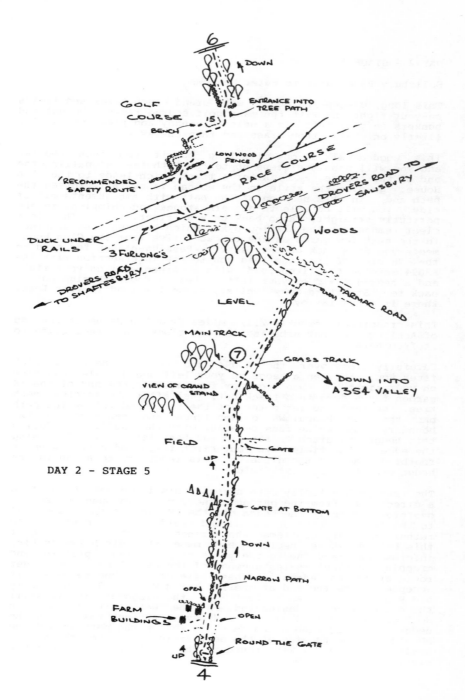

6

DOWN

GOLF
COURSE

ENTRANCE INTO
TREE PATH

15

BENCH

LOW WOOD
FENCE

RACE COURSE

'RECOMMENDED
SAFETY ROUTE'

DROVERS ROAD TO
SALISBURY

DUCK UNDER
RAILS

WOODS

3 FURLONGS

DROVERS ROAD
TO SHAFTESBURY

LEVEL

TARMAC ROAD

MAIN TRACK

7

GRASS TRACK

DOWN INTO
A354 VALLEY

VIEW OF GRAND
STAND

FIELD

GATE

DAY 2 - STAGE 5

UP

GATE AT BOTTOM

DOWN

NARROW PATH

OPEN

FARM
BUILDINGS

OPEN

ROUND THE GATE

UP

4

DAY 2 - STAGE 6

Salisbury Racecourse to Water Meadows

This long, descending path, with grand beech trees and fields on your right and with the many golf course trees, bushes and bunkers on your left, is a welcome, shady and pleasant stroll, firstly on chalk, then grass and then chalky soil.

This wooded walk is one mile long but it seems much shorter and you will soon see steps up to the 18th tee, signalling the end of the course. After a track which leads to the Club House, go over the stile in the wooden fence that crosses the path and, in this section of the path with embankments either side, you will be able to discern stones and chippings in the perfectly straight, high bank on your right. This is a clear remnant of the Ackling Dyke which becomes less distinct in the next few yards as the tarmac drive from the Club House meets you from back on the left. Passing-places for cars on the RH side of the lane lead you to the intersection with the A3094 Harnham to Wilton road, with a garden wall on your right and a hedged field on your left. Here a Footpath sign points back to "Stratford Tony" whilst, along the road to your left, there is a bus lay-by.

This crossing is exactly 2.1/2 miles from Old Sarum at the end of Ackling Dyke but urbanization has blocked a direct route to it from here.

Carefully cross over the A3094 and go onto the track which faces you, between a hedge on your left and a chalet bungalow on your right. Don't go any further than the end of the RH garden fence down this track but, just after the massive beech tree, go past the far corner of the fence and follow the path past the other bungalows' garden fences and then alongside the boundary hedge which runs parallel with the A3094. Follow this hedge and ditch to its end and bear left, still following the edge of the field, to four birch trees and a twin-sleeper footbridge across the ditch. This leads you to a gap in the hedge and into the next field.

The true path actually cuts across this field and the next in a direct line from the garden corner, via this opening (see an overgrown stile in the hedge on the RH side of this opening) to the far LH corner of the second field. However, the rather military gentleman who arranged for the positioning of this bridge where neglect had made the ditch impassable, informed me that, due to the years of ploughing, planting and cropping without re-instatement of the path line, the longer route around the edges of these fields had become generally accepted since the end of the 2nd World War. See how easily old Rights of Way can be lost - and the diagonal path is still the official one, designated on the Definitive Map as Path No.2 as late as 15/2/94. However, through the gap in the hedge, you now have a choice - to follow the path around the RH side or the LH side of the next field. For those of a hesitant nature - I went round to the right, passing under O/H electric wires on the way.

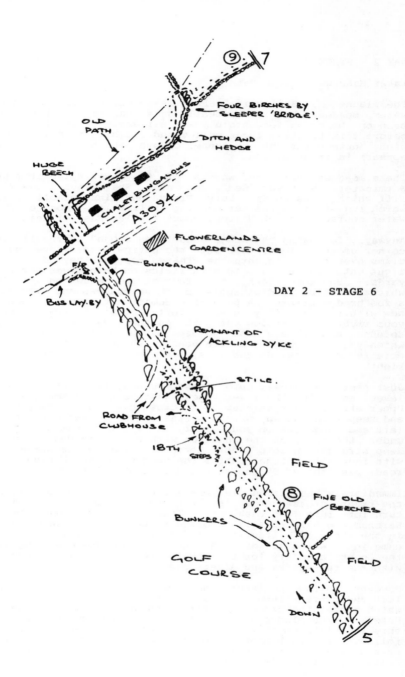

⑨ 7

FOUR BIRCHES BY
SLEEPER 'BRIDGE'.

OLD
PATH

DITCH AND
HEDGE

HUGE
BEECH

CHALET BUNGALOWS

A3094

FLOWERLANDS
GARDEN CENTRE

F/B

BUNGALOW

DAY 2 - STAGE 6

BUS LAY-BY

REMNANT OF
ACKLING DYKE

STILE.

ROAD FROM
CLUBHOUSE

18TH
STEPS

FIELD

⑧ FINE OLD
BEECHES

BUNKERS

GOLF
COURSE

FIELD

DOWN

5

DAY 2 - STAGE 7

Water Meadows to Town Path

The planned A36 Salisbury By-Pass is calculated to cross these
water meadows when it eventually gets started - but this has
been on the cards for untold years already.   If it is built
before this treatise turns yellow and crumbles to dust in your
hand, just go through the tunnel or over the bridge, whichever
appears in front of you.

These meadows carry the waters of the River Wylye from near
Warminster, the River Sem from near Shaftesbury, the River
Till which rises on Salisbury Plain and innumerable streams
which run off from the surrounding chalk hills. Most of these
water courses meet at Wilton, about 3 miles East of here.

Anyway, following the hedges and trees around to the far left
corner of this field, turn into the narrow, shady opening and
climb over the stile onto the clearer footpath beyond.   Bear
right onto the raised path with fields on both sides for a few
yards.   You soon reach a tributary of the Nadder on your left
which is filled by drainage from these meadows and over which
a footbridge brings the path from Bemerton village.   Keep on,
now with the tributary on your left and an old track down on
your right.   Follow the path on the levee (elevated flood
defence) and you are soon joined by the Nadder itself, after
which you come to some modern houses which are protected by a
more recent grassy defensive system and a sluice gate on your
right.

Just past the gateway onto these mounds, the path leaves the
levee and joins the lower track just before it emerges into
Upper Street, West Harnham.   Cross over to the RH pavement
and keep straight on, with a stream in the grassy ditch on the
left and bungalows on your right.   The stream soon passes
under the road, at the junction with Berkshire Road, and you
keep straight on into Middle Street.   Follow the stream, now
with football pitches behind the hedges on the LH side of the
road, past the No 55 bus stop and Constable Way on your route.

Immediately the stream disappears under a brick garden wall on
the right, cross over to the left and, passing Old Mill House,
turn left into Town Path.   This public footpath from West
Harnham to Salisbury is reported to be the most used footpath
in the whole of Wiltshire.   I did mention it, didn't I?   You
came into Wiltshire at Toyd Clump, having been walking along
the County boundary for the upward, boring mile after the fork
with the two-stones and after Toyd Farm.

However, follow the tarmac lane, past the Three Crowns on your
left and a tree-lined play area on your right. to the footpath
which passes the stone and flint chequered front of the Mill
Hotel.   The plaque on the wall gives loads of the history of
this fine 12th Century building so, after you've read it, keep
following the path around the Mill buildings until open fields
present fine views across the water-meadows to the magnificent
Salisbury Cathedral itself.

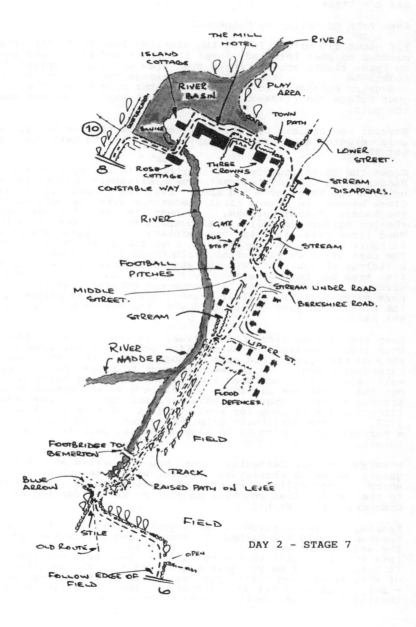

RIVER

THE MILL HOTEL

ISLAND COTTAGE

RIVER BASIN

PLAY AREA.

TOWN PATH

10

8

LOWER STREET.

ROSE COTTAGE

THREE CROWNS

STREAM DISAPPEARS.

CONSTABLE WAY

RIVER

GATE

BUS STOP

STREAM

STREAM UNDER ROAD

FOOTBALL PITCHES

BERKSHIRE ROAD.

MIDDLE STREET.

STREAM

RIVER NADDER

UPPER ST.

FLOOD DEFENCES.

FIELD

FOOTBRIDGE TO BEMERTON

TRACK

RAISED PATH ON LEVÉE

BLUE ARROW

FIELD

STILE

OLD ROUTE

OPEN

DAY 2 - STAGE 7

FOLLOW EDGE OF FIELD

6

DAY 2 - STAGE 8

Town Path to Salisbury Cathedral

For about 1/2 mile, follow the elevated Town Path with fenced
meadows on your left and, over the track and tree-lined fence
on your right, you can enjoy the view which so inspired John
Constable   You will pass drainage controls on the left
and gated entrances to fields on either side of the Town Path
just before the track on the right gives way to a stream below
the path.

Several comfortable benches will tempt you to stop but you are
only minutes away from journey's end so try to wait until you
get there.

Cross the footbridge over the Northern tributary of the River
Nadder which now hurries past Queen Elizabeth Gardens to meet
up with the River Avon and then, past the gardens of the fine
Close houses, to make a final rendezvous with the main part of
the Nadder at East Harnham.   Go past the three benches facing
the footbridge and follow the footpath to the pavement of Mill
Road (Town Mill, that is, not Harnham).   Passing houses and
Harcourt Terrace on the left, go over the stream bridge, with
the park still on your right, into Crane Bridge Road.   The
buildings on your left are the abandoned City Hospital (unless
the area has been developed by the time you arrive), so keep
straight on, passing the telephone and conveniences by the car
park on your right.   After Crane Lodge, the next bridge spans
the River Avon just before it joins the Northern tributary of
the Nadder.

Keep straight on along Crane Street to the traffic lights and
turn right, passing the unique 14th Century timber-framed book
shop on the corner, and walk through High Street Gate into the
Cathedral Close.   It seems strange to think that the stone
wall which still encircles much of the Close was built to keep
out the rebellious citizens of Salisbury who caused so much
trouble to the clergy, including violent robbery, that Edward
III granted a licence for the building of this gated wall in
1327.   This particular gate, being nearest to the city, had
a portcullis which could be lowered during periods of greatest
unrest.

Straight on into Cathedral Close, you now arrive at the fenced
green, known as Choristers' Square, with a telephone box from
which you can call for rescue or collection or just announce
to the world that you have completed the first leg of "The
Cranborne Chase Path".

Keeping to the straight line of your arrival into the Close,
cross over into the Cathedral grounds and follow the path to
the magnificent West Front.   Such is the unique history of
this fine Cathedral that many volumes have been written about
it but, if you find yourself a seat and turn to the other side
of this Stage map, I'll give you a few of the salient points
- but, firstly, a bit of information about Mompesson House in
Choristers' Square which is well worth a visit.

66

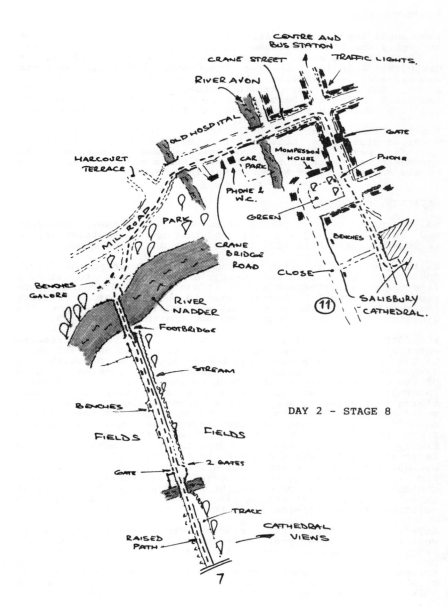

CENTRE AND
BUS STATION

CRANE STREET

TRAFFIC LIGHTS.

RIVER AVON

OLD HOSPITAL

GATE

HARCOURT
TERRACE

MOMPESSON
HOUSE

PHONE

CAR
PARK

PHONE &
W.C.

PARK

MILL ROAD

GREEN

CRANE
BRIDGE
ROAD

BENCHES

BENCHES
GALORE

CLOSE

⑪

SALISBURY
CATHEDRAL.

RIVER
NADDER

FOOTBRIDGE

STREAM

BENCHES

DAY 2 - STAGE 8

FIELDS

FIELDS

GATE

2 GATES

TRACK

RAISED
PATH

CATHEDRAL
VIEWS

7

MOMPESSON HOUSE:

The magnificent Queen Anne town house residence of the staunchly Royalist Mompesson family stands on the North side of Choristers' Square, ornately gated and fenced, facing the Cathedral. Inside this fine 17th Century building, there are mementoes of the families who have lived in this friendly house, including some charming water colour paintings by the immensely talented Barbara Townsend who lived here from the mid-19th Century until her death, at the age of 97, in 1939.

The important Turnbull collection of 18th Century English drinking glasses is housed here together with many rather touching personal items, photographs and furniture of the fortunate residents of this lovely house before it was given to the National Trust by Denis Martineau in 1952.

SALISBURY CATHEDRAL:

Salisbury is the only Cathedral to have been planned, designed and built as a single entity and that partly explains why it is so singularly beautiful in its style and proportions.

Building started in 1220 through the inspiration of Bishop Poore, (not to mention the clergy's desperation to get away from the cold, waterless and fractious site of Old Sarum where stood the original Cathedral, next to the troublesome military fortress). The West Front was completed by 1258 but the cloisters and Chapter House were not finished until 1285.

The 404ft high Cathedral's masterpiece, the 'upward rushing waterfall' of the spire, was added between 1285 and 1320 when, to the original low tower was added 6,400 tons of additional stonework. The original main columns on the internal corners of the crossways are visibly bent by the strain. Massive internal vaulting and girder arches are helped by external flying buttresses to support this crowning glory. The latest major repair work has cost millions of pounds but this isn't a one-off event. Repair and restoration has continued non-stop since the 13th Century. It is carried out to this day by the highly skilled and inventive Department of Works under the leadership of the Clerk of Works to the Dean and Chapter, Roy Spring, a man of immense skill who enjoys, and is touched by, his responsibility to the Cathedral in its vastly historical context. I appreciate Mr Spring's great help to me in explaining his observations which led to his dating these building stages differently to the official guide book.

Anyway, as you sit here, reading these notes, ignore the questioning looks at your muddy boots and unkempt appearance. Enjoy your moment of glory. After all, most of the assembled populace in the Close will be tourists from Japan, America or Europe who will probably have paid thousands of yen, dollars or whatever to visit the Cathedral. You have enjoyed a fine walk on the way, and have got here for next to nothing.

DAY 3 INTRODUCTION

Salisbury Cathedral to Berwick St John

Leaving Salisbury's wonderful Cathedral, you walk through West Harnham and out on the Old Blandford Road to join the Drovers Road.   This high level route is meant to keep your cart wheels or your hooves dry for practically the whole of the 3rd Day until you descend into Berwick St John at journey's end.

All day today, you will have easy walking with fine views over the Nadder Valley on your right and down into the Ebble Valley on your left.

You pass Salisbury Racecourse again, but parallel to the track this time and, after crossing the Wilton Road, you follow the unsurfaced Drovers Road, without turning off to left or right, uninterrupted except for a visit to Chiselbury Camp, until you descend into Berwick St John

	STAGE	MILES	TOTAL
1	Salisbury Cathedral to Bishop's Walk	1	1
2	Bishop's Walk to Old Shaston Drove	1.25	2.25
3	Old Shaston Drove to Racecourse	1.50	3.75
4	Racecourse to Hut Bottom Bend	3.25	7
5	Hut Bottom Bend to Chiselbury Camp	2	9
6	Chiselbury Camp to Middle Down	3.75	12.75
7	Middle Down to Gallows Hill	1	13.75
8	Gallows Hill to Whitesheet Hill	1	14.75
9	Whitesheet Hill to Berwick St John	0.75	15.50

If at all possible, save Day 3 for a clear, dry period because the long distance views on both sides of the Drovers Road into the Ebble and Nadder Valleys deserve mist-free days.   And, as I found to my cost, some of the ruts in the unsurfaced Drovers Road caused by years of use by wheeled vehicles, tractors and carts do not drain very quickly and present an extra hazard. It's not that the puddles are particularly deep or dangerous. It's just that tacking to avoid them can add, or so it seems, another mile to the journey to Berwick St John.

Ordnance Survey Map No 184 is the only one that you will need today and it will help you to work out what all of the distant hills, valleys and villages are which you will see from this high level walk.   The Wilts and Dorset bus along the Ebble Valley from Berwick St John to Salisbury is the No 29 but, if you use it, make sure your boots are clean.

DAY 3 - STAGE 1

Salisbury Cathedral to Bishop's Walk

Reluctantly leaving the wonderful West Front of the Cathedral,
go out onto the pathway which runs alongside the Cathedral's
Works Department and parallel to the Sports Field on the other
side of the road.   At the end of the Close, turn left through
Harnham Gate and continue down DeVaux Place to its end.   Turn
right into St Nicholas Road with St Nicholas Hospital over the
opposite brick and flint wall.   After Nos 10 and 12, which
are perched right on the edge of the River Avon, go over the
13th Century bridge which, as carved on its stone, was widened
by Bishop Bingham in 1774.   This bridge was the major access
into Salisbury for everybody who came here from all the Chase
villages and towns - all linked together by Ackling Dyke and
the Turnpike road.

After the second bridge, bear right into Harnham Road but not
before calling into positively the last shop on our route. The
Post Office on the corner of Ayleswade Road.   This shop isn't
as remote as some which we will visit on "The Cranborne Chase
Path" but, even so, all local Post Offices need our support as
well.

Now, continue along the pavement (I know your route is marked
on the map as being up the middle of the road but, when I try
to squeeze the lines onto a pavement, they aren't as clear as
they should be), passing the Rose and Crown on your right and,
near the end of the road on your left, a line of four thatched
cottages.

Carefully cross over the A3094 Netherhampton Road, by the two
telephone boxes, and turn up Old Blandford Road opposite.   As
you walk up the hill, look back occasionally for fine views
down onto the Cathedral.   After the turning on the right for
the "Salisbury Lawn Tennis Club" and Chiselbury Grove on your
left, the left pavement runs out where a long staircase shoots
up into the trees.

On your right, next to the Grasmere Close turning, a signed
Footpath leads onto the lower slopes of the tree-covered bank
but do not take this turning.   Instead, keep on up the right
pavement past a fenced-in transmitter mast until you come to a
wide and grassy area on your right.

At the signpost, turn right across this open space and go past
the wooden fence section, turning left onto a high level path
with wooden panel fences of the houses on the left and thickly
wooded slopes on the right.   This is Bishop's Walk and, apart
from the convenient benches, the first thing you will notice
is the granite commemorative stone which acknowledges the gift
of this Walk and adjacent slopes from John Wordsworth D D, the
Bishop of Salisbury 1885 - 1911.   After this stone, follow
the path, past the steps up into Bishop's View Estate on your
left and more benches with fine views back to Salisbury.

70

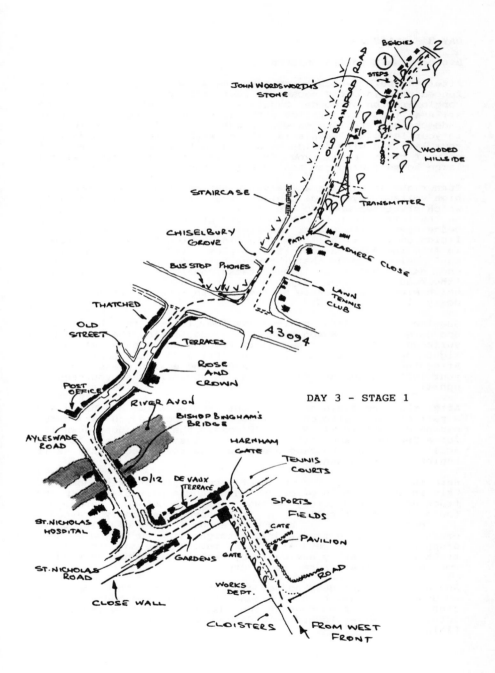

DAY 3 - STAGE 1

DAY 3 - STAGE 2

Bishop's Walk to Old Shaston Drove

After the path which turns down the slope on your right and a
fenced path into the houses on your left, you soon arrive at a
conglomeration of wooden barriers.   Turn left over the step
stile at the "Avon Valley Path" disc, now going uphill, past
paddocks and stabling on your right and a wide path going off
to your left.   Keep straight on, with houses and gardens on
your left and with fields belonging to "Parsonage Down Estate"
on your right, until you drop down to a T-junction with a
large house facing you behind a 6ft panel fence.

Turn right and, after a few yards between hedges and under the
high voltage overhead cables, you arrive in an open field
which stretches down to the A354 Blandford to Salisbury road
on the left. Keep to the chalk and grass track next to the RH
hedge down to the end of the field where, with openings into
fields on your right, you join Old Shaston Drove which comes
in from the A354 on your left.   Commonly known as "Salisbury
Way", Defoe records that, between here and the Whitesheet hill
end, as the valley villages' tracks come up to meet this road,
"the road often lyes very broad, and branches off insensibly,
which might easily cause a traveller to lose his way".   Don't
worry, I'll guide you.

Shaston, as in Shaston Drove, is the old name for Shaftesbury
and dates back to Saxon times.   So, follow the old tarmac
surfaced lane, with a secondary track running parallel on its
right, up past Nos 1 and 2 with "Private" woods behind them.
After the cottages, there is a hedge and a wide grass verge on
your left and another dual track on your right as you keep on
uphill.

After the open field on your right, you pass two old barns and
a pair of gates also on the right, just before you pass under
overhead electric wires. At "Braemar" the track goes downhill
for a few yards and, after a gate and the turning into "Little
Acre", the track becomes overgrown, narrower and grassy as it
begins to ascend again.

Here for the first time, we meet the triple-track phenomenon.
This is where wheels of carts have dug a pair of ruts in the
track and, with a lovely grassy space in between, horses and
those who are struggling on foot have eventually created a
3rd, central rut.   With such a combination of ruts, it is
often difficult to find a dry, straight line to follow without
dropping into cart ruts or a horse rut.   The majority of the
track is only easily navigable by walkers, without tacking to
port and starboard, when it is dry.

Anyway, with the deep hedges closing in from both sides, keep
on uphill towards the high ground as gaps in the hedge on your
right offer glimpses down to the Western end of Salisbury and
across the valley towards Old Sarum and the edge of Salisbury
Plain.

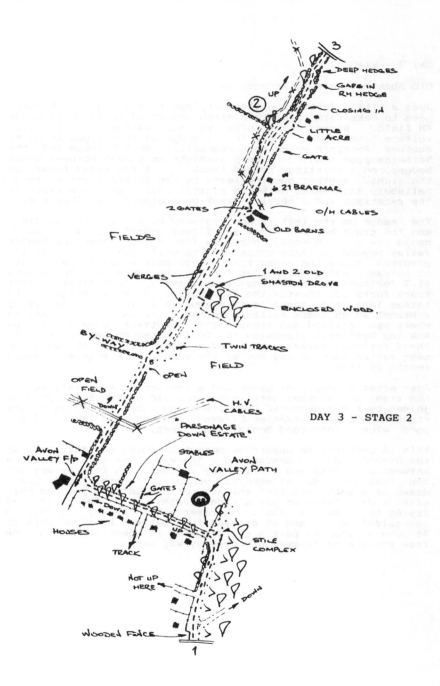

DAY 3 - STAGE 2

3

DEEP HEDGES

GAPS IN
RH HEDGE

2 UP

CLOSING IN

LITTLE
ACRE

GATE

21 BRAEMAR

2 GATES

O/H CABLES

OLD BARNS

FIELDS

VERGES

1 AND 2 OLD
SHASTON DROVE

ENCLOSED WOOD.

BY-
WAY

TWIN TRACKS

FIELD

OPEN

OPEN
FIELD

DOWN

H.V.
CABLES

"PARSONAGE
DOWN ESTATE"

AVON
VALLEY F/P

STABLES

AVON
VALLEY PATH

GATES

DOWN

STILE
COMPLEX

HOUSES

UP

TRACK

NOT UP
HERE

DOWN

WOODEN FENCE

1

73

DAY 3 - STAGE 3

Old Shaston Drove to Racecourse

Just a little further on the left, you find a wide track which goes to Bake Farm opposite a ditch-protected entrance into the RH field.   Higher still, after you have passed under the high voltage lines again, a gap in the hedge on your right leads to another Footpath which goes downhill to West Harnham and the Netherhampton Road.   Keep straight on though between dense hedges, on a twisting, rutted track.   A few yards later, on the right, another opening leads to the furthest extremity of Salisbury Racecourse as white plastic rails mark the start of the racetrack and a service track goes around the other side.

The hedge on the left is now replaced by a strip of woodland and the track becomes wider and firmer underfoot. With the RH hedge now quite sparse, there are fine views across the Nadder Valley beyond the Racecourse and the Golf Course.   As you progress along the wider track, you pass a lay-by and a pair of entrance gates which lead through the fence onto the course at 7 furlongs and 6 furlongs respectively.   Just after another track forks off towards the Racecourse, you will recognize the tarmac lane which comes in from your left, followed shortly by a branch which leads directly to the track rails.   This is where you arrived and crossed the Racetrack to walk down the Ackling Dyke path alongside the Golf Course on Day 2, near to the 3 furlongs marker.   Today, keep straight on, past the next rutted section and out of the woods, to a sparsely hedged length of track.

Just after a couple of gates and a section of iron railings to the right and another gate into the field on the left, you are joined by the Racecourse Grandstand and other buildings on the right and Coombe Nurseries Caravan Park on your left - with a good, wide tarmac road beneath your feet.

This is probably an opportune moment to point out that most of the Drovers Road is designated a "By-Way". The main difference between a By-Way and a Bridleway is that, on this By-Way you can "use any kind of wheeled vehicle - whether it is horse drawn or a motor vehicle" whilst, on a Bridleway you can only walk, ride a horse or use a pedal cycle.   The point I am trying to make is that, wherever this By-Way crosses a recognized road - and it crosses four between here and Berwick St John - you can park a car provided it doesn't obstruct the free passage of farmers or other By-Way users.

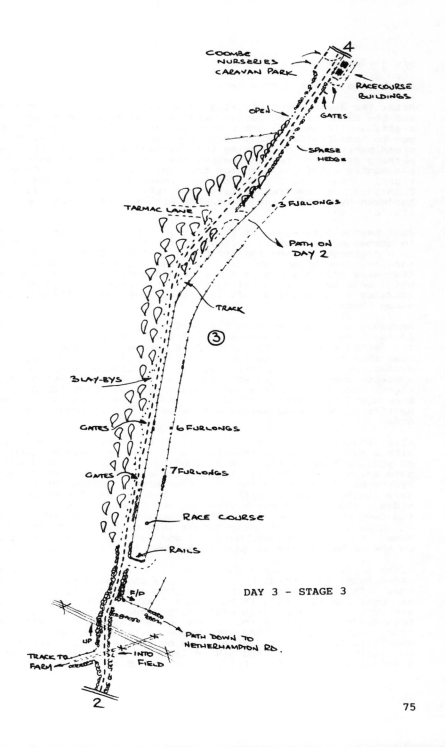

COOMBE
NURSERIES
CARAVAN PARK

RACECOURSE
BUILDINGS

OPEN

GATES

4

SPARSE
HEDGE

3 FURLONGS

TARMAC LANE

PATH ON
DAY 2

TRACK

③

3 LAY-BYS

GATES

6 FURLONGS

GATES

7 FURLONGS

RACE COURSE

RAILS

F/P

DAY 3 — STAGE 3

PATH DOWN TO
NETHERHAMPTON RD.

UP

TRACK TO
FARM

INTO
FIELD

2

75

DAY 3 - STAGE 4

Racecourse to Hut Bottom Bend

After the grass verge, parking areas and stabling on your left
and the Racecourse buildings, stables and Parade Ring on your
right, a wire fenced, beech bedecked area on your right brings
you to the Stratford Tony to Wilton crossroads.   Carefully
cross over the road, passing the "By-Way" signpost in the car
parking area, and leaving behind the tarmac surface which had
pleasantly eased your way for the last 1/2 mile.   On your
right, a gate leads into the vast beech wood of the "Forestry
Commission Harewarren" whilst the left side of the track is
bordered by a thin line of beeches with a wire fenced field on
its far side.

Just beyond both sides of the track, low banked ditches begin
to accompany our route.   They are too high above the track to
be a drainage ditches for the Drovers Road and, pondering this
for some time along the way, I came to the conclusion that
they were probably dug as a "ditch and bank" to prevent cattle
which were being driven along this long track through ancient
woodland from wandering off into the thick woods. I'm probably
wrong though.

Anyway, the track becomes firm and stony with many deep holes
for a while as you progress past 3/4 mile of the Harewarren to
the second road crossing, from Bishopstone to Wilton.   Cross
over this road, passing the right corner gate and the "By-Way"
arrows, onto a similar stony but firm section of track between
a deeper beech strip on your left and the "Harewarren" on your
right. This is more like the woods through which the Drovers
Road would have been carved all those years ago - deep and
heavily wooded with hardly a glimpse of the valleys on either
side.

After another 1/2 mile, you come to a clearing on your right
with a gate into the Harewarren and a wide, tree-lined turning
on your left which leads to a wooden section of fence and a
gate across the path. All four routes are signed as Bridleways
by the discs nailed to the LH corner post.   Straight on now,
on a rougher surface with hedges, beeches and fences on both
sides, there are clearer views on the LH side as we have left
the deep woodland behind.   After openings into the RH fields,
which have become slightly higher than our path and block the
view, the track becomes narrower and bends a bit whilst gaps
in the LH hedge give us good views down into the Ebble valley.

After a turning on the right which leads up to a grass-covered
water tank and a Bridleway which goes down between beeches on
your left, keep going a little further and you will be able to
see over the RH fields to Salisbury Plain.   It is now grassy
and rutted underfoot with wider verges and sparse hawthorns on
both sides.   After another hidden water tank on the left, the
track continues to a bend with woods on both sides and a horse
jump into the RH part. After this bend, the track straightens
out again with bushes and a wire fence on either side and with
a thin line of beeches striding over the rise on the right.

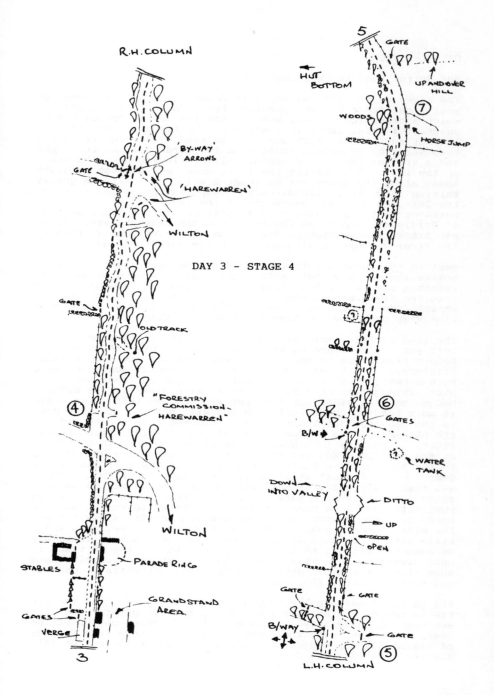

R.H. COLUMN

'BY-WAY' ARROWS

GATE

'HAREWARREN'

WILTON

DAY 3 - STAGE 4

GATE

OLD TRACK

④

"FORESTRY COMMISSION HAREWARREN"

WILTON

STABLES

PARADE RING

GATES

VERGE

GRANDSTAND AREA

3

5

GATE

HUT BOTTOM

UP AND OVER HILL

⑦

WOODS

HORSE JUMP

⑦

⑥

GATES

B/W

⑦ WATER TANK

DOWN INTO VALLEY

DITTO

UP

OPEN

GATE

GATE

B/WAY

GATE

⑤

L.H. COLUMN

DAY 3 - STAGE 5

Hut Bottom Bend to Chiselbury Camp

The trees on the left become more dense again and the hedge on
your right leads to an opening into the high field next to
which a generator rumbles away inside its aerial bedecked hut.
Just after this, there is a stile in the trees on the left but
I'm not sure where it is supposed to lead. So, ignore it and
keep straight on with a small wood 100 yards away on the right
and a similar small wood immediately following over the fence
on the left. Just before the first wood, you can see straight
ahead along the drove for at least a mile. After a grassy
turning into the LH field, with deep hawthorns and trees on
the left and more old hawthorns on the right, the track grows
narrower until you arrive at a junction with a wider section
of Bridleway from Broad Chalke to Compton Chamberlayne. There
are tracks to the Drovers Road from every village in both of
the river valleys, giving access to the markets in Salisbury.

Next to the opening into the field on the near right corner, a
notice reminds you that, although you are now on a By-Way, the
turnings off it are Bridleways.   Anyway, a farm gate leads
into the field beyond the deep trees and hawthorns on the left
whilst, over the wire fence on the far RH corner, there is a
fine view over Compton Down to Chiselbury Camp.

The road surface improves again for a while, with trees on the
left and a wire fence on the right, until a deep RH verge with
hedges brings you to the leaving point of the zig-zag crossing
Bridleway.   It bears off sharp left, through woods and past
more submerged water tanks, whilst our journey continues, as
ever, straight on to a rutted track with grass up the middle,
hedges on both sides and a deeper wood on the left. The route
is more bending for a while and you will notice, through gaps
in the hedges, that the track has crossed from the LH side to
the RH side of the ridge, now giving clearer views to the
right.   You are in highwayman territory now.   This stretch
of the Salisbury Way was the haunt of Cunning Dick who used to
tether his horse in Gurston Wood, 1/2 mile South of Chiselbury
Camp.   An old oak still bears the staple to which his horse
was tied - allegedly.   Now, with deeper wooded strips on both
sides, go past a farm gate which turns sharply into a field on
your left next to a pine-lined wood. The whole route suddenly
opens out into a wide, airy panorama as the track divides and
the wire fence on your right turns away to a horse jump and a
stile with a Footpath arrow. Choose the LH track if it is dry
because the view is better into Knapp Down but the RH track is
much grassier.   This wide section is where a Turnpike gate
once stood with cross-dykes to discourage attempts by coaches
and carts to avoid the gate.

The LH fence has a horse jump into the valley and, as the two
tracks merge, the RH wire fence has a pair of gates. The Iron
Age camp of Chiselbury is beyond the RH fence, on top of the
steep escarpment over the Nadder Valley.   There is a display
of regimental cap badges on the Fovant side which was cut into
the chalk by soldiers during the 1914-18 war.

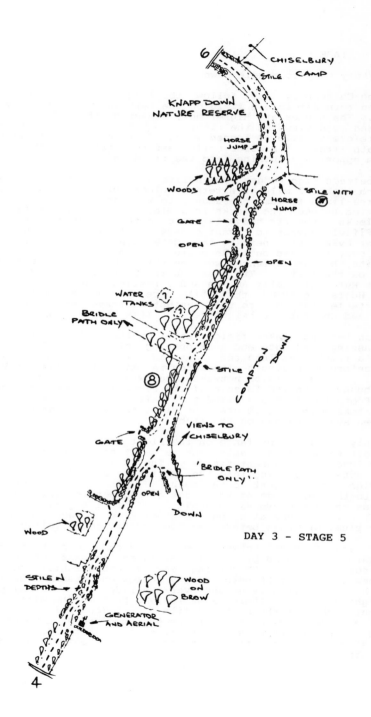

6

CHISELBURY
STILE CAMP

KNAPP DOWN
NATURE RESERVE

HORSE
JUMP

WOODS

GATE

STILE WITH
⑦

GATE

HORSE
JUMP

OPEN

OPEN

WATER
TANKS   ⑦

BRIDLE
PATH ONLY

⑦

STILE

⑧

VIEWS TO
CHISELBURY

GATE

'BRIDLE PATH
ONLY'

OPEN

DOWN

WOOD

DAY 3 - STAGE 5

STILE N
DEPTHS

WOOD
ON
BROW

GENERATOR
AND AERIAL

4

DAY 3 - STAGE 6

Chiselbury Camp to Middle Down

Leaving Chiselbury Camp, follow the long, straight track past
a gated turn off into a field on the left and a lay-by on your
right.   The hedges are higher now, denser on the left but with
gaps and good views on the right.   A gap in the RH hedge,
just before a strip of fenced woodland, reveals a stile with a
Footpath arrow. A similar stile next to a gate into the woods
stands opposite a turning into the field on your left.

Now, between high hedges, you arrive at a long, straight, firm
stretch with 1/2 mile of alternate blocks of chicken sheds and
fir tree-lined fields, presumably to keep any risk of fire and
infection between the blocks to a minimum.   After the last of
the blocks, the fir hedge turns round the corner as the road
from Fifield Bavant to Fovant crosses your path.   There is
another By-Way sign next to the gate into the RH field.   Now
cross over the road onto the quite firm, but hole-filled track
opposite, between a fenced wood on the right and a banked open
field on the left.   The house on the right is the modernised
Fovant Hut, originally an inn and a resting place but, in 1812
Colt Hoare reported that "it once proved a useful and
comfortable 'taberna' to the benighted traveller over these
bleak and uninhabited heights".   It's not that bad, is it?

Keep on between banked fields, still on the right of the ridge
and passing a RH gate and a LH opening into two fields. On the
left, a track goes into the woods as our route divides again,
just before a Footpath sign which is nailed to a bush on your
right.   The division between the twin tracks is grassy and
then bushy.   On the LH edge of the secondary track, Bridleway
and Footpath discs are fixed to a pair of old posts and, as
the tracks merge, there are fine views through the opening and
between sparse bushes on the right.

Suddenly, there is no fence on the right and, in a wide gap in
the left hedge, a farm gate and a small gate with a Footpath
arrow lead into adjacent fields.   The LH side is still hedged
and, after an opening into the RH field, a border hedge goes
off right at a tangent to our path.   The route now crosses
back to the left side of the ridge giving better views to your
left as the hedge breaks up again.   After a gate in the LH
hedge, a track runs along on its other side, between the hedge
and a clump of trees before the edge of Prescombe Valley.

A few yards further, between hedges, you come to a crossing of
Footpaths, indicated by a yellow arrow on the near left corner
fencepost.   The LH turning is clear and downhill, between
beeches whilst the RH path is very narrow and grassy, between
high hedges as it goes up and over the ridge.   Keeping
straight on again, there is scarsely a bush in the wire fence
on your right for the next 1/2 mile.   You will pass a few
openings, an arrowed stile in the RH fence and a five-barred
stile in the LH fence as you progress to a spot with views on
both sides where the track divides into two again at a wider,
open area.

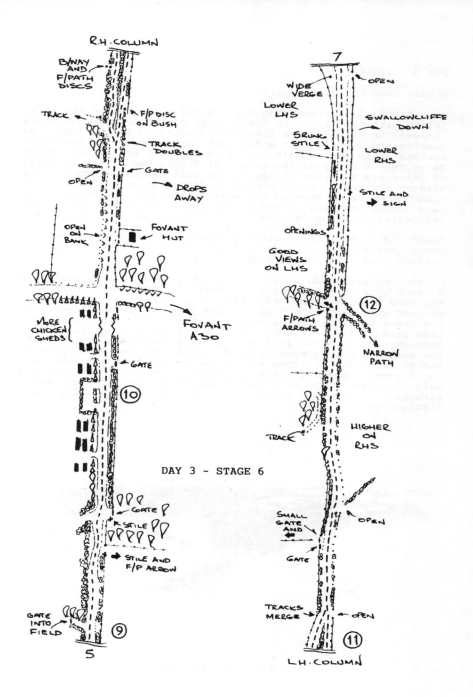

R.H. COLUMN

B/WAY AND F/PATH DISCS

TRACK

F/P DISC ON BUSH

TRACK DOUBLES

OPEN

GATE

DROPS AWAY

OPEN ON BANK

FOVANT HUT

MORE CHICKEN SHEDS

FOVANT A30

GATE

(10)

DAY 3 - STAGE 6

GATE

R.STILE

STILE AND F/P ARROW

GATE INTO FIELD

(9)

5

7

OPEN

WIDE VERGE

LOWER LHS

SWALLOWCLIFFE DOWN

5 RUNG STILE

LOWER RHS

STILE AND SIGN

OPENINGS

GOOD VIEWS ON LHS

(12)

F/PATH ARROWS

NARROW PATH

TRACK

HIGHER ON RHS

SMALL GATE AND

OPEN

GATE

TRACKS MERGE

OPEN

(11)

L.H. COLUMN

DAY 3 - STAGE 7

Middle Down to Gallows Hill

With Middle Down presenting a wonderful view down on the left,
follow either of the twin tracks with hawthorns and deep grass
between them, passing a five-barred stile in the LH fence, an
opening and a stile with a Footpath arrow in the RH fence and
another stile on the left (in that order) before the tracks
merge near a copse on the slopes of Middle Down.   An array
of gates and 5-barred stiles on the left lead you onto a level
stretch of track, still with wire fences on either side, but
with the RH fence turning off behind a wooded area where there
is a convenient lay-by and a high-fenced enclosure with some
unlabelled building lurking within behind equally high gates.

Immediately after this, with twin gates on the near LH corner,
cross over the Alvediston to Ansty road, which has a vicious
hairpin bend just out of sight on the Swallowcliffe scarp.

On the opposite side of the road, the track is very wide with
a beech wood on either side.   There is a narrow opening into
the wood on your right and, next to a farm gate, there is an
arrowed stile into the field on the left.   Beech trees line
the track until a grass lined track turns off right, next to a
farm gate in a wire fenced field.   A narrow path turns down
between hedges on the left and, after a section of twin track,
the route is accompanied by good views over the wire fence on
the RH side, a wire fence with a few sparse bushes on the left
and a gentle uphill track with grassy verges for the next 1/4
mile.   Then, after an opening into fields on the right and a
gate and five-barred stiles into the field on the left, keep
straight on.

Middle Down. This Page

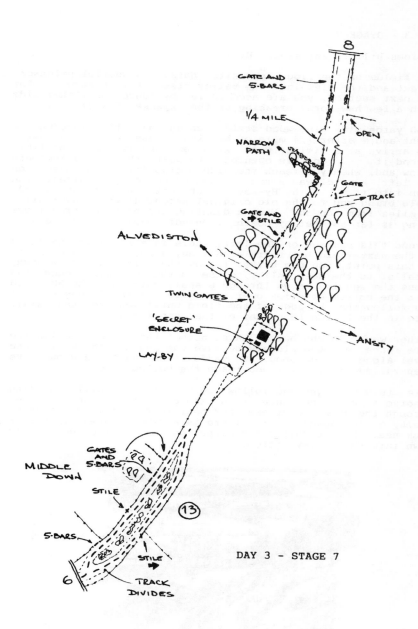

GATE AND
5-BARS

1/4 MILE

OPEN

NARROW
PATH

GATE

TRACK

GATE AND
STILE

ALVEDISTON

TWIN GATES

'SECRET'
ENCLOSURE

LAY-BY

ANSTY

GATES
AND
5-BARS

MIDDLE
DOWN

STILE

5-BARS

STILE

TRACK
DIVIDES

DAY 3 - STAGE 7

DAY 3 - STAGE 8

Gallows Hill to Whitesheet Hill

The fields on the ridge opposite have a wonderful patchwork
effect and the view into the valley crescent is superb.   For
the next section, you are accompanied by fences on either side
with a few hawthorns breaking up the expanse of wire.

A 50 yards wide pine wood strides up and over the ridge on the
right and, after 1/4 mile of bending, grassy and rutted path,
you arrive at a similar wood with an opening into the field
beyond it.   On this opening's LH post, there is a Footpath
arrow and, when you reach the wide, scrub-filled passageway on
the left, a Bridleway arrow on the LH corner post directs you
down into it.   The By-way, which continues straight ahead,
would bring you to the old original ascent at Whitesheet Hill,
97 miles from London.   What a daunting prospect for travellers
going as far as that by coach or on horseback - or on foot.

Beyond this passage on the left, there is a stile in the fence
of the next field but there aren't any direction arrows on it.
At this point, you can either follow the Bridleway arrow down,
parallel to the deep gulley, close to the left wire fence, and
cross the gulley to go through a small gate into the RH field
near the bottom or climb over the stile off the By-way so that
you follow the LH edge of the field until you meet that small
gate in the bottom LH corner of the same field.

Either way, in the bottom LH corner of the field, follow the
wire fence, not too closely because the vague path is nice and
level along a ridge about 30 yards from the fence around the
deep valley side, until you reach the bottom LH corner.

Here, turn up right and follow the wire fence uphill, passing
a horse jump in the fence, to a farm gate at the top.   Go
through the gate, no arrows, and bear left to follow the deep,
chalky gulley downhill.   There is a slumped arena in the LH
bank near the top whilst the slope on the right drops steeply
down into the valley bottom.

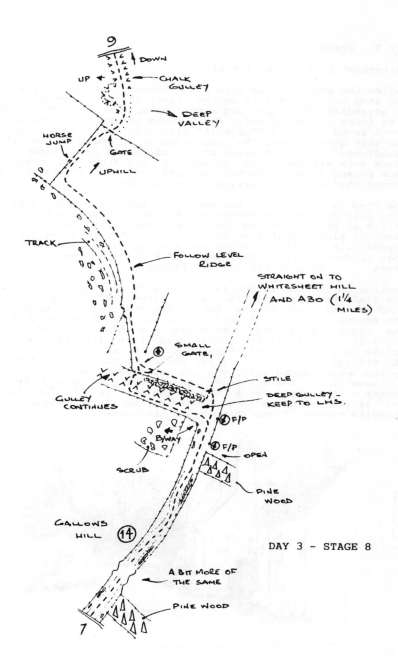

9

DOWN

UP → ←CHALK GULLEY

→ DEEP VALLEY

HORSE JUMP

GATE

↑ UPHILL

TRACK

FOLLOW LEVEL RIDGE

STRAIGHT ON TO WHITESHEET HILL AND A30 (1¼ MILES)

SMALL GATE

STILE

GULLEY CONTINUES

DEEP GULLEY — KEEP TO LHS.

F/P

BYWAY

F/P

OPEN

SCRUB

PINE WOOD

GALLOWS HILL ⑭

DAY 3 - STAGE 8

A BIT MORE OF THE SAME

PINE WOOD

7

DAY 3 - STAGE 9

Whitesheet Hill to Berwick St John

Follow the chalk gulley with the embankment on the LH side and
the drop into the valley on the right, through a beech wood as
it straddles the track, and across an open area to arrive at a
wire fence at the bottom.   Go through the gate and follow the
track round,   past a "Footpath" sign which points back uphill,
and walk quietly past the fine stone-built house on the left -
"Woodlands", with its stone stable block and large kennels.   A
track goes off into the valley on the right and, after you
have passed between the two gate pillars, you will be on level
tarmac road until you arrive in Berwick St John.

The road is lined with beeches, birches and maples, together
with ditches and wire fences all the way.   Beyond a protective
circle of beeches in the field on your left, there is a fine
clump of pine trees up on the hill.   This is Horse Hill and
anyone with serious literary pretensions will instantly notice
that it does a superb impression of Winnie the Pooh's Six Pine
Trees.   Keep an eye out for Tigger!

Passing an opening in the fence on your right and a gate into
the field on your left, follow the tree-lined lane past a gate
into another field on the right.   You are now going uphill for
the second, and last, time today as you pass some old barns on
the right and turnings into a couple of houses on the bank on
the left.   After the cattle grid of the last RH house, you
arrive in Church Street, Berwick St John and turn left towards
the village centre.   If you parked at the side of the road
by the hedge-topped wall, you are now back at your car but, if
you have to get the bus back, the stop is just around the next
corner - the stone block outside the barn next to The "Talbot
Inn" if you are going to Salisbury or the stone shelter on the
opposite corner if you're going to Shaftesbury.

The Talbot Inn, Berwick St John. This Page

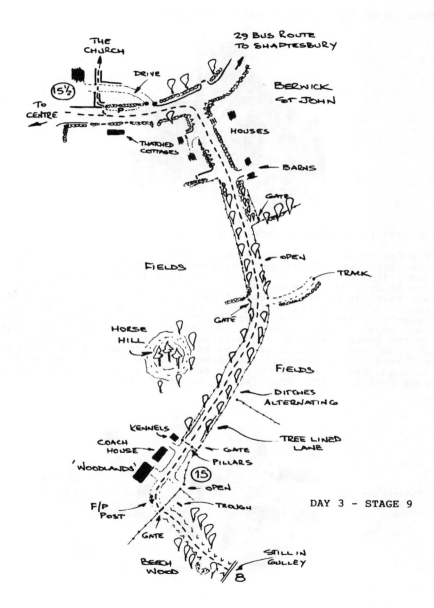

THE CHURCH

29 BUS ROUTE TO SHAFTESBURY

DRIVE

(15½)

BERWICK ST JOHN

TO CENTRE

P

HOUSES

THATCHED COTTAGES

BARNS

GATE

FIELDS

OPEN

TRACK

GATE

HORSE HILL

FIELDS

DITCHES ALTERNATING

KENNELS

TREE LINED LANE

COACH HOUSE

GATE

'WOODLANDS'

PILLARS

(15)

OPEN

DAY 3 - STAGE 9

F/P POST

TROUGH

GATE

BEECH WOOD

STILE IN GULLEY

8

ST JOHN THE BAPTIST - BERWICK ST JOHN

The Church of St John the Baptist was built around the end of
the 15th Century and contains some beautiful medieval tracery
and a fine painting, on wood, of William de Wykeham, Bishop of
Winchester, dated about 1600. In the South and North transepts
are sections of stone arches from the local chantry which were
recovered during the restoration of a local farm and these now
house fine stone effigies of knights in medieval armour.   In
the South transept there is the effigy of John Hussey whilst,
in the North transept is Robert Lucy's effigy.   By the will
of John Gane, a rector who died in 1746, the bell of St John's
was rung every evening, from eight o'clock to a quarter past,
between September and March to guide parishioners and workers
back home from the outer reaches of Cranborne Chase.

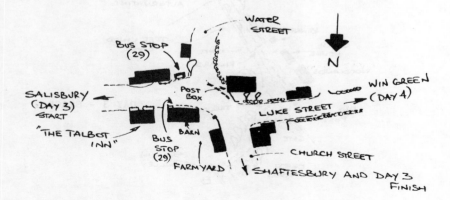

Plan of the village, showing arrival and departure points

DAY 4 INTRODUCTION

Berwick St John to Shaftesbury Abbey

High excitement today with a visit to the highest point on the
whole of Cranborne Chase - Win Green, 911 feet up on the most
scenic part of the whole of the Ox Drove.   This is the
alternative drovers road from Shaftesbury to Salisbury, where
the valleys are precipitous and the views over the Chase are
magnificent.   From the Salisbury Way, our view of the Chase
was foreshortened by this other ridge but, from here, the line
of vision takes in far distant horizons.   I'll let the stone
direction plinth at the top of Win Green explain more fully.

From Win Green, the route goes through lush pastures, arable
land and ancient woods and includes a luxurious stroll along
most pleasant country lanes on our way to the Saxon hill town
of Shaftesbury.

This latter part of the walk is liable to provide glimpses of
groups of roe deer, quietly grazing the field margins or, not
so quietly, crashing into the undergrowth as they sense your
approach.

	STAGE	MILES	TOTAL
1	Berwick St John to Monks Down	1.25	1.25
2	Monks Down to Ox Drove	1	2.25
3	Ox Drove to Elliott's Shed	1	3.25
4	Eliott's Shed to Charlton	1	4.25
5	Charlton to Lower Coombe	1	5.25
6	Lower Coombe to Middle Coombe	0.75	6
7	Middle Coombe to Dockham Bottom	1.25	7.25
8	Dockham Bottom to A350	0.75	8
9	A350 to Shaftesbury Abbey	0.50	8.50

Today, you will need Ordnance Survey maps 184 and 183, in that
order, and the timetable for the Wilts and Dorset bus No 29 to
renew your acquaintance with Peter the driver - friend and
confidante to his regular passengers.   Also, if you think you
may need an early escape at Ludwell, the No 26 timetable.

Really though, with only 8.1/2 miles to walk today, there will
be ample time to "stand and stare" so an early departure isn't
something that should be considered.   An early arrival in
Shaftesbury would allow time to visit the Abbey or the Museum
or to stroll around the delightful Park Walk and garden.

DAY 4 - STAGE 1

Berwick St John to Monks Down

Starting from the bus stop, turn up Luke Street, with the post
box adorned cottage on the LH corner, and head uphill past the
lych gate of St John the Baptist's on your right.   If you've
been to visit the church first, come out through the lych gate
and turn right.

Passing cottages on the left, with Church View and a gate into
the field on the right, continue slightly uphill, passing more
cottages, a long stone barn and a fine stone-mullioned house
on the left as you approach a junction with another lane which
comes in from your right.

Follow your bending lane past the many buildings of the large
farm on the opposite RH corner.   At the second farm gate on
your left, a pair of signed Footpaths go off across the field,
either of which would return you to Berwick St John via Water
Lane.   Keep straight on, passing steps up to the shed on
your right and following the banked fences on either side of
the lane, until you arrive at Upton Lucy house - remember the
effigy of Robert Lucy in St John's.

As the lane becomes hedged on the left and begins to descend
slightly into a shady gully, take the turning on the right, a
signed Bridleway on a tree-lined corner.   Now, with a fenced
field on your right and a hawthorn hedge and trees on the LH
field margin, start along the firm, but chalky and stony track
past a collection of broken old eyesore trucks - about which,
I am informed, the Council is able to do nothing at all.

Anyway, these are soon passed and the track becomes very badly
rutted, passing a grass covered water tank on the left.   The
field on the right is now unfenced.   The roe deer which I
mentioned in today's Introduction can often been seen on the
margins of this large field, close to the wooded slopes ahead,
but even when they are hiding you will probably see hoofprints
in this track.

Descending slightly now, you pass a couple of trees behind the
hedge on your left and cross the bottom, probably boggy, part
of the field, before beginning the ascent of the track which
will soon bring you to the topmost spot of Cranborne Chase.

On the way up, you will have superb glimpses of Monks Down and
Winklebury Hill Fort through the 50 yards wide open section on
the left and, as you leave the field, with the high banked and
wire fenced pine woods on your right, stay on the main track
when a grassy track goes into the woods.

The fenced scrub wood on your left as you ascend is home to a
horde of pheasants, if that's the right collective noun, but
don't let their squawks and sudden lunges from the undergrowth
startle you.

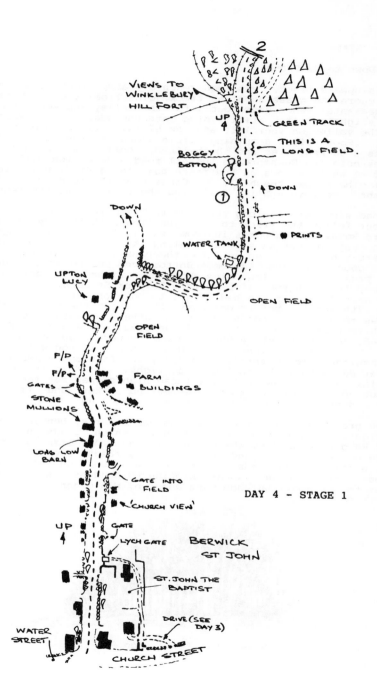

VIEWS TO
WINKLEBURY
HILL FORT

2

GREEN TRACK

THIS IS A
LONG FIELD.

UP
4

BOGGY
BOTTOM

① ↓ DOWN

DOWN

●● PRINTS

WATER TANK

UPTON
LUCY

OPEN
FIELD

OPEN FIELD

F/P
F/P

GATES
STONE
MULLIONS

FARM
BUILDINGS

LONG LOW
BARN

GATE INTO
FIELD

'CHURCH VIEW'

DAY 4 – STAGE 1

UP
4

GATE

LYCH GATE

BERWICK
ST JOHN

ST. JOHN THE
BAPTIST

DRIVE (SEE
DAY 3)

WATER
STREET

CHURCH STREET

DAY 4 - STAGE 2

Monks Down to Ox Drove

On this upward track, you soon reach a grassy clearing on the
right where the grass woodland track joins from below.   Here,
the pheasants' fence goes down into the valley and your track
bends slightly left, still rising into the edge of the woods
with the valley on your left and the hillside trees up on your
right.   Soon, after a turning circle around a tree, the track
becomes a banked, tree and bush-lined, hollow-way which then
emerges onto the Rushmore to Ludwell road. Here, you will see
a pair of white arrows on the fence post and a Bridleway arrow
pointing back down the hill.   Cross over the road, close to
the bank, and turn uphill, following the bank around the bend.

The road sign points along the road to Rushmore and Berwick St
John but follow the track to the junction with the "By-Way to
Tollard Royal" which comes in from the left on the top ridge.
Before setting out on your walk along the Ox Drove, for this
is where you join it, go up onto the bank in front of you and
have a good look into Ashcombe Bottom over on the other side.
This presents a glorious view and, even without the delights
to come, is worth the climb up from Berwick St John.   The Ox
Drove served drovers who had to get to Downton Market and fair
every 12th April, but it was busy throughout the rest of the
year as this track connected with others heading for the
Hampshire ports - routes for beef supplies to the Navy.   Even
in 1805, an average of 16,000 live cattle were supplied to the
Navy.   Carry on along the Ox Drove which, as you will see,
is "Unsuitable for Motors", and enjoy the farmland views into
'Higher Berry Court Bottom' on your right.   This is not an
official name but, as we follow these high slopes for the next
mile or so, it deserves to be recognized later and, from up
here, Higher Berry Court Farm dominates the view.

As you progress, by turns downwards and upwards, bending left
and right, you will pass a farm gate which leads onto the
upper RH downs and from where you will have your first glimpse
of the Day's target beyond the ridge straight ahead of you.
After a stile which leads into the private woods on the slopes
on your left, the next upward sloping RH bend brings you ever
closer to the small but dominant woods of Win Green.

Win Green, 911 feet. Page 94

92

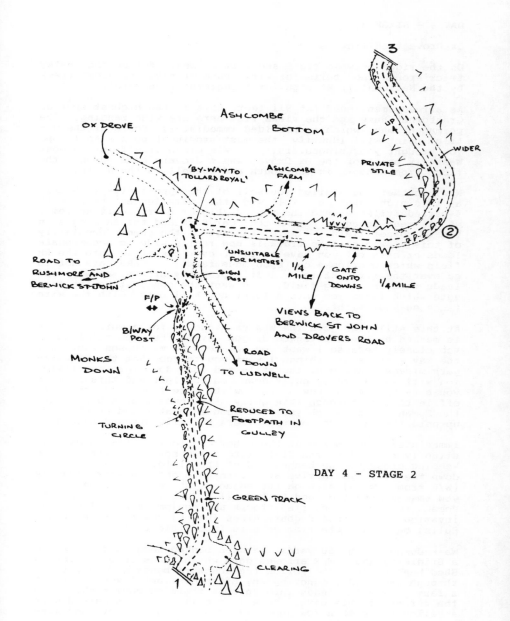

OX DROVE

ASHCOMBE BOTTOM

3

UP

WIDER

'BY-WAY TO TOLLARD ROYAL'

ASHCOMBE FARM

PRIVATE STILE

2

ROAD TO RUSHMORE AND BERWICK ST·JOHN

'UNSUITABLE FOR MOTORS'

SIGN POST

¼ MILE

GATE ONTO DOWNS

¼ MILE

F/P

B/WAY POST

VIEWS BACK TO BERWICK ST JOHN AND DROVERS ROAD

MONKS DOWN

ROAD DOWN TO LUDWELL

TURNING CIRCLE

REDUCED TO FOOTPATH IN GULLEY

DAY 4 - STAGE 2

GREEN TRACK

CLEARING

1

93

DAY 4 - STAGE 3

Ox Drove to Elliott's Shed

On the ridge between right and left slopes, follow the chalky
track around the perimeter wire fence or take the green track
by the National Trust sign for "Wingreen" (one word).

As already mentioned, at 911 feet, this is the highest spot on
Cranborne Chase and the views from here are wide-ranging. The
permanent map which is provided immediately South of the O S
trig point will identify the most prominent points so I hope
you brought your binoculars. Win Green itself is the most
Westerly point of the Ox Drove, where drovers came up onto the
ridge from Ashmore in the South and Ludwell in the North.

Now, whether you availed yourself of the opportunity to picnic
at this high spot or followed the wire-fenced track with
4-barred stiles around the top of "Higher Berry Court Bottom",
we all meet up again beyond the Car Park and the farm gate in
the LH corner field. Here, because of the summer popularity
of this viewpoint, the track is now really wide to accommodate
loads of cars but you have to climb over the stile into the RH
field which overlooks our eponymous farm. Take care not to
go over the first stile. It's probably broken, anyway, and
leads into the wrong field. You want the one next to the farm
gate which leads you onto a faint downhill path with the wire
fence on your right.

At this stile, we join the Wessex Ridgeway for a while. This
is marked by the two-legged dragon symbol but don't follow it
too closely because I want you to keep to my chosen route all
the way - there are things I want you to see that the Ridgeway
path misses. Stand by the stile and look down into our field.
You will see a grassy gully down on the left and this is what
you have to aim for now. Follow the wire fence and then turn
off left to go through this gully - a remnant of a branch off
the Roman road, which you will soon encounter and which leads
up onto the Ox Drove for travellers to Salisbury and London.

Immediately you emerge at the other end (only a few yards), go
slightly right down the field into a few scrubby hawthorns and
keeping close to the hedged end of the field. A few yards
down the hill, you arrive at a farm gate and a Wessex Ridgeway
(W/R from now on) sign on the adjacent stile. Over the stile,
you emerge onto the road to Ludwell. This is a remnant of the
Roman road which carried troops and equipment all along the
invasion route from Badbury Rings (Day 6) towards Bath (Aqua
Sulis) but its route from here is impossible to follow.

Walk downhill for 60 yards, between banked hedge and fence, to
a Bridleway and a W/R arrowed gate which leads into Elliott's
Shed beechwoods. Follow the downward bending, muddy track
through the woods, ignoring any offshoots, until you arrive at
a farm gate which leads into an open field on your right. On
the corner of this gate, there is a stile which is marked with
a yellow Footpath arrow and a W/R sign. Ignore both and keep
going downhill into a narrowing, bush-lined hollow-way.

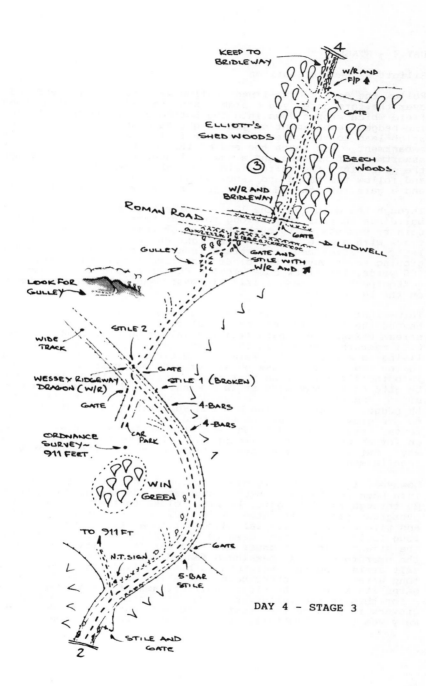

KEEP TO
BRIDLEWAY

W/R AND
F/P

ELLIOTT'S
SHED WOODS

GATE

③

BEECH
WOODS.

W/R AND
BRIDLEWAY

ROMAN ROAD

GATE

→ LUDWELL

GULLEY

GATE AND
STILE WITH
W/R AND

LOOK FOR
GULLEY →

STILE 2

WIDE
TRACK

GATE

WESSEX RIDGEWAY
DRAGON (W/R)

STILE 1 (BROKEN)

GATE

4-BARS

4-BARS

ORDNANCE
SURVEY ~
911 FEET.

CAR
PARK

WIN
GREEN

TO 911 FT

N.T. SIGN

GATE

5-BAR
STILE

DAY 4 – STAGE 3

STILE AND
GATE

2

95

DAY 4 - STAGE 4

Elliott's Shed to Charlton

Follow the deep, scrub-lined hollow-way down to its end and,
over the farm gate, you emerge into the RH corner of an open
field which slopes down into the bottom of the valley. Follow
the hedged embankment on your right to a short line of trees
which lead to the gate out of this field. Still following the
embankment, you reach the end of this next field with a vast
assortment of troughs and a row of fenced trees. Go through
the gate into the third field, a much longer one this time,
and follow the hedge and fence on your right, passing troughs
and a gate into the RH field, just before you leave our field.

Through the gate into the last, shorter field, the cluster of
buildings on your left belong to Manor Farm and, in the hedged
corner, you now go through the last of these gates into a wide
track with a wire fence on the right and a row of trees on the
left. Sometimes, this track is narrower because of rapidly
growing scrub but it was clear last time I came this way. In
100 yards, the track comes to the Charlton to Ludwell road, at
a "Footpath Win Green 1.1/2" signpost and with a fenced house
on the LH corner.

Turn right onto the road, with two huge oak trees in the field
beyond the fence facing you. Follow the road down to where a
stream passes underneath from the valley on your right. You
will meet this stream further down the valley, working for its
living as a water cress farm. Beginning to rise now, keep
to the road past a house on either side and past the farm gate
into the first field on your left. Take note of the second
LH gate as you may need it in a minute. With hedges on both
sides, and after only a few yards, look out for a stile in the
LH hedge. This carries W/R and Footpath arrows but tends to
be overgrown - as does the confined path beyond it. If the
route, between the LH hedge and the RH fence is clear, carry
on for about 250 yards altogether, climbing two stiles on the
way, until you emerge, over a last stile, at the end of your
'confinement'.

However, if the route is overgrown, and this won't be unusual,
turn back to the gate which I suggested you may need instead.
Go through the farm gate, keeping close to the hedge with the
overgrown path on its other side. Climb over the broken stile
and wire fence in its far RH corner to arrive at the top of a
long field which slopes down to the valley bottom where lurks
the stream which ran under the road earlier. Still alongside
the overgrown route, passing a fenced wood on the left and the
exit stile from the overgrown path, the field drops down to a
long array of watercress beds. This is where the small stream
earns its keep. The clear chalk streams of the Nadder Valley
- for this is the valley which you are entering - have enabled
growers to produce the most delicious watercress for many,
many years and, hopefully, for many more years to come.

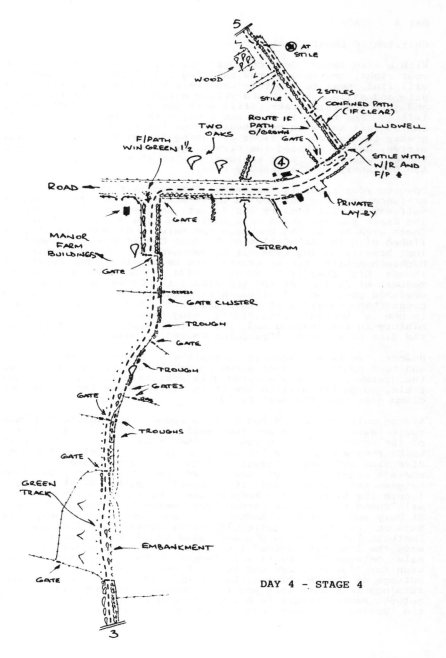

5

WOOD

🛑 AT STILE

STILE

2 STILES
CONFINED PATH
(IF CLEAR)

LUDWELL

ROUTE IF
PATH
O/GROWN
GATE

TWO
OAKS

STILE WITH
W/R AND
F/P ♠

④

F/PATH
WIN GREEN 1½

ROAD

PRIVATE
LAY-BY

GATE

MANOR
FARM
BUILDINGS

STREAM

GATE

GATE CLUSTER

TROUGH

GATE

TROUGH

GATES

GATE

TROUGHS

GATE

GREEN
TRACK

EMBANKMENT

GATE

3

DAY 4 - STAGE 4

DAY 4 - STAGE 5

Charlton to Lower Coombe

With a wire fence down on your left and the hedge still up on
your right, continue to the tapering end of this field and you
will find, next to a watercress farm building on your left, a
gate and stile with W/R and yellow arrows. Go over the stile
and join the farm track, still with the watercress beds on the
left.   The track is firm and stony with a drop into the beds
on the left and with an embankment on the right.   Passing a
grassy turning on the right and going around a bend, you soon
arrive, having crossed the stream again as it runs to join the
Nadder where the track emerges between stone cottages, at the
A30 Salisbury to Shaftesbury road.

Down on your right is the Grove Arms and, if its late morning
or lunchtime, why not pop in for a snack or a coffee.   You're
half-way to Shaftesbury and a rest isn't out of the question.
The Grove family, which once dominated the Northern Cranborne
Chase area around the Donheads and Berwick St John, is closely
linked with the Arundell's of Wardour Castle and both families
lost heavily during Cromwell's Commonwealth.   Originating in
Buckinghamshire, the Wiltshire line began with John, nephew of
Thomas, High Sheriff of Bucks in 1434.   Constantly producing
Members of Parliament for the area, the Groves maintained an
enviable position.   In 1882, Sir Thomas Grove's son joined the
great Chase families of Grove and Pitt-Rivers by his marriage
to one of General Pitt-Rivers daughters.   The family's
history is fascinating and, for a full appraisal, I recommend
the fine treatise on "Cranborne Chase" by Desmond Hawkins.

However, we have a journey to finish.   So cross over the A30
and turn uphill for just a few yards before turning right, up
the grassy bank, to a kissing gate next to a farm gate. In the
field, go up the hill to the stile in the hedge facing you and
climb over into the next field.

At the gate at the RH end of this hedge, the Wessex Ridgeway
route leaves us so we are lone explorers again.   At the top
of the next field, go through another kissing gate onto a path
which runs alongside a leylandii hedge.   Follow the same
direction and keep straight on through this estate, emerging
where a signed "By-Way" goes down the track on your right
between the houses and the Ludwell County First School.
Ignore the By-Way but, keeping the School wall on your right,
walk round to join the tarmac lane which runs down to Donhead
St Mary and Donhead St Andrew.   Now, passing the only farm
gate on the left, opposite Old School House, and from where a
Footpath (still on the O S map) used to go across the field to
save the long trek around the lane, continue downhill for 1/4
mile, between high banks with hedges on top.   After a high
sign for "The Donheads and Lower Coombe", turn left.   Past a
cottage on the RH corner, the sign for "Lower Coombe" and
turnings into both left and right houses, drop downhill, still
between banked hedges to a high, fenced field on your left and
the turning to "Lower Coombe Farm" on your right.

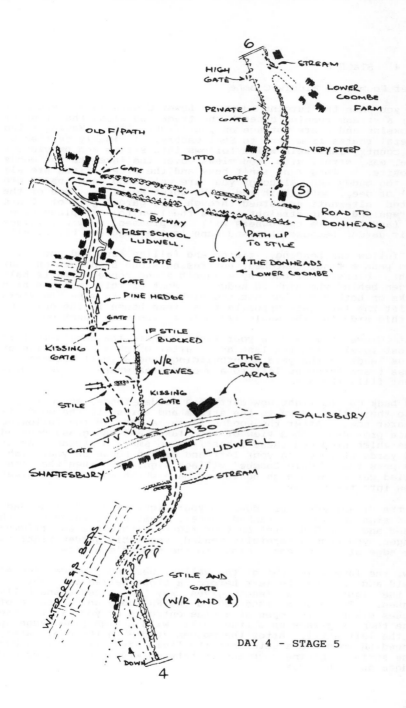

DAY 4 - STAGE 5

99

DAY 4 - STAGE 6

Lower Coombe to Middle Coombe

As you pass the turning down to Lower Coombe Farm, you will hear a stream running beneath the track and along the front of Brookside and Clare Cottage on your right. Having tried several routes from here to Shaftesbury, I finally settled on the country lane walk which follows this stream and provides a fine, easy stroll with good views over the lakes to the woods opposite. This lane isn't busy and the alternatives are all far too muddy and, although you are well shod, some parts are full of deep, soft, thin mud - the worst sort. One of the tested alternatives turned through this garden gate of Clare Cottage and went straight across the lawn to "Shipland Lane" but (and I'm sure the owners will be pleased) we won't invade their garden because Shipland Lane is the boggiest bit of all.

So, follow the bending, rising and falling lane and you will soon pass a fine, thatched, buttressed stone barn down on your right, closely followed by a superb stone house which is half hidden behind the high RH hedge. Most of this lane has high banks on both sides but not too high for you to miss the views whilst the farm gate opposite this stone house is the only one on this side for the whole 1/2 mile to the next junction.

Past Grove Farm yard on your right, where the barn's roof is almost level with the lane and, after which a combination of gates leads to the yard's outbuildings and a small orchard, a grass track turns up left to a wooded area where a lovely pine scent fills the air.

The bank on the right now carries a wooden fence, so your view into the valley, down to the stream and across to the woods is clearer now. After the wooden fence, a gate in the following fence provides a good view of two lakes and the grass covered dams which produced these lakes from so small a stream. After 100 yards of woods on your left and banked hedge on your right you pass the "Middle Coombe" village sign, and then the stone walled garden of a high house and barn which must have a great view into the valley.

At the crossroads, turn down to your right with a "Cul-de-Sac" road sign on the far, banked corner. Passing cottages on both sides and "The Old Barn" on your right, with gates and trimmed hedges, you pass a carefully tended vegetable garden right on the edge of the stream - close to the Nadder's source.

Now, the lane rises out of the valley, passing a wooden fenced field and gate on the left before a stone-walled barn whilst, on the right, a wire fence gives way to a hedge and holly bushes. Two houses stand behind the RH hedge and a couple of houses stand in the open at a wide entrance on your left. The lane then zig-zags up a steep hill with a high pine hedge up on the left until, after the wooden stable in the many-gated, fenced LH wood and a gate into the field after it, the tarmac lane surface begins to break up between wide grass verges and hedges on both sides.

DAY 4 - STAGE 6

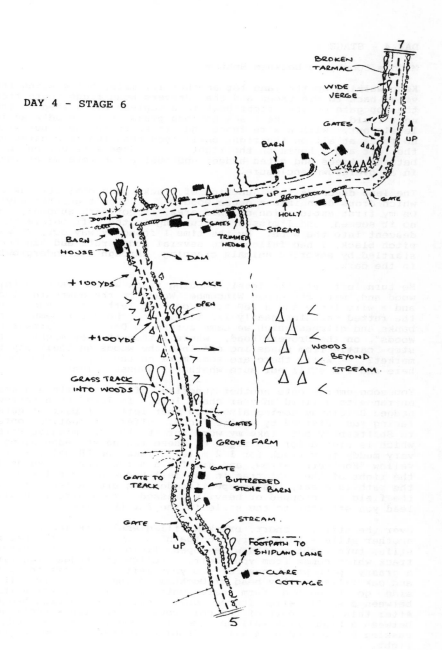

BROKEN TARMAC

WIDE VERGE

GATES

UP

7

BARN

GATE

UP

HOLLY

GATE

DOWN

R GATES

STREAM

BARN
HOUSE

TRIMMED HEDGE

DAM

+100YDS

LAKE

OPEN

+100YDS

WOODS
BEYOND
STREAM.

GRASS TRACK
INTO WOODS

GATES

GROVE FARM

GATE TO
TRACK

GATE

BUTTRESSED
STONE BARN

GATE

STREAM.

UP

FOOTPATH TO
SHIPLAND LANE

CLARE
COTTAGE

5

DAY 4 - STAGE 7

Middle Coombe to Dockham Bottom

Keep walking up the lane for another 1/2 mile, not missing the
views back to Win Green and the Drovers Road ridge route from
the top gate on your right next to a topless brick shed in the
next field. The track now has grass up the middle as it
levels out, with a wire fence and trees on the left but with
no fence at all on the right until you pass two farm gates on
the left and a house on the right. Keep straight on, now
between trees and gated hedges and past a concrete water tank
in an overgrown enclosure.

The lane descends to a junction of tracks, the most obvious of
which drops down into a dense wood. "Don't go that way!"
On my first exploration of this area, it got dark suddenly, or
so it seemed, and I missed the turning to the left before this
descent into the wood. By the time I found my way out, it was
pitch black, I had fallen into several muddy ruts and had been
startled by assorted animals crashing through the undergrowth
in the dark.

So turn left onto the level, bending track which precedes this
wood and, with the dense Wincombe Woods on the downward slope
and a wire fence and a few trees on your left, continue along
the rutted path for nearly 1/2 mile. Do you remember the
banks and ditches which we came across on Day 3 in "Harewarren
Woods" on the Drovers Road, where I thought they might be to
stop cattle from wandering off into the woods on their way to
market? Well, there are some more on the edge of the woods
here and I'm still not sure whether I guessed right.

You soon emerge onto another junction of tracks with a grassy
entrance to a field on your sharp left, followed by a narrow,
hedged Bridleway coming also from your left. A pair of gates
facing you, divided by a wire fence, offer alternative routes
to Shaftesbury but, take my word for it, the "Permissive Path"
which is signed for the right of these two gates leads along a
very muddy farm track for 1/2 mile. Take the LH gate, with a
yellow "Footpath" arrow, and aim for a point about 10 yards to
the right of the last tree in the left hedge of this field. If
the path is clear, these specific details are wasted but, if
the field is cropped or heavily grassed, this direction will
lead you straight to the stile in the far LH corner.

Over the stile, a short, bracken filled enclosure leads you to
another stile - both carry "Footpath" arrows. Over the second
stile, turn right in the wide open field and join the grassy
track which comes from your left. Follow the hedge, ignoring
a grassy path which goes off to your left, and cross the pine
and oak filled valley head of Dockham Bottom. Up the other
side, go through a farm gate onto a bridleway which runs
between a small, wire fenced golf course and a high hedge.
After this first part of the golf course, the track continues
between a high brick wall on the left and the same RH hedge,
passing a 5-barred gate with a "Public Footpath" arrow on your
right.

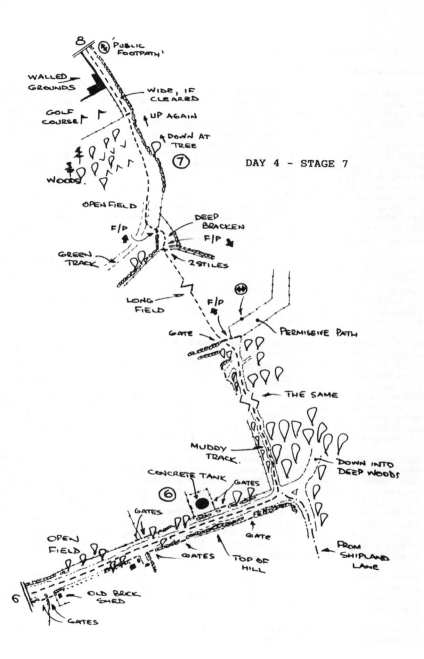

DAY 4 – STAGE 7

DAY 4 - STAGE 8

Dockham Bottom to A350

At the end of the brick wall, go through a squeeze stile next
to the gate into a wide open, grassy field which drops down on
the left - note the fine cedar.   From here, you can see
Melbury Beacon over on the left, ahead of you.   At 864 feet,
it isn't much below the height of Win Green and it marks the
Western edge of Cranborne Chase.   You will be crossing this
high downland on Day 5, hopefully tomorrow as it's a glorious
walk.   For now though, follow the RH hedge, passing a gate, a
tree, a holly bush and a cattle trough on your way to another
squeeze stile next to a gate and a wooden-fenced enclosure at
the end of this field.   Through the stile, the valley beyond
is clothed with beeches, oaks and some fine pines.   Back up
the other side, go through the gate with broken hinges and no
stile onto an enclosed track with a hedge on the right and a
gated, wooden-fenced field on the left.

Where the left hand field hedge joins our track, the stile is
overgrown and the gate is missing, (or it was last time), but
this is a significant spot for all that.   Where the wooden
fence is divided by a gate on the left and the track crosses
to Eastleaze Farm on your right, you now cross over the County
boundary from Wiltshire into Dorset, staying in Dorset for the
final two Days of our journey.

Go through the squeeze stile ahead of you into a grassy field
which is home to a sleek, inquisitive horse.   Be careful
that he doesn't come and lean on you.   Follow the enclosing
leylandii hedge around to the right, aiming for a stile which
is half-way along the wooden fence which borders the private
drive to Eastleaze Farmhouse.   If, like me, you find the bulk
of an advancing horse to be somewhat intimidating, go over the
gate onto the drive before it can get to you. Either from the
gate or stile, turn left up the drive and leave by the gate
or squeeze stile next to the two field gates at its end.

You now emerge onto a road with an electricity sub-station on
the left, just before a gate into the hedged field.   Follow
the road, using the pavement where provided, first passing the
banked beech hedge on your right and passing gates into the
last fields on left or right.   You are now on the outskirts
of Shaftesbury and, after Pound Lane, you pass the cemetery's
lych gate on your left.   Shaftesbury's Church of England
First School on your right and a row of bungalows on your left
bring you, past Fairlane, to the wide grass verges of the A350
road from Blandford to Shaftesbury.

Keep straight on past a post box and cross over on the pelican
crossing to the other side.   Turn up the A350 and, with rows
of houses on your left, cross St Rumbolds Road and continue to
the next left, Coppice Street.

Turn into Coppice Street and prepare yourself for your visit
to Shaftesbury - at the end of your pilgrimage from Salisbury.

104

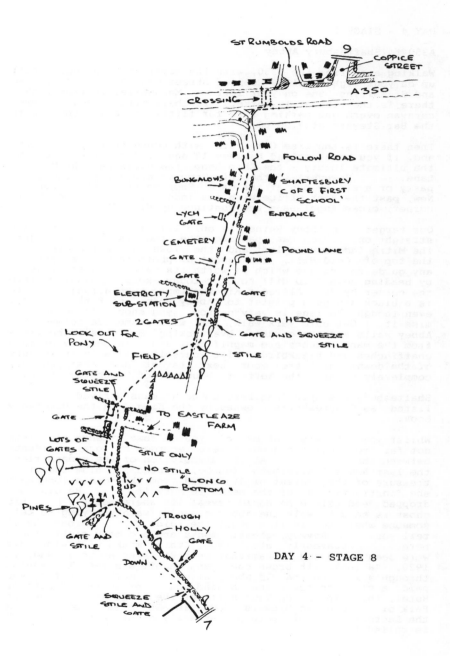

DAY 4 - STAGE 8

DAY 4 - STAGE 9

A350 to Shaftesbury Abbey

Walking away from the A350, with the Royal British Legion hall
up on your right, follow Coppice Street past Old Boundary Road
and St Martins Lane on your left.   Meanwhile, on your right,
there is the old cattle market, football pitches and a summer
caravan overnight parking site for fifteen caravans (book with
the Bar Steward at 7.00 pm).

Then there is the free Car Park with convenient conveniences
and, if you have arrived between 12 and 2.00 or after 5.00 pm,
the ultimate luxury - the Chip Shop, two doors past St Martins
Lane.   However, if the Chip Shop is closed, you can get a
pasty or a sticky bun at the Cake Shop on the next LH corner.
Now, past the Post Office with its indoor telephones on the RH
corner, cross Angel Lane and continue up High Street.

Our target, the Abbey Ruins, is only 1/4 mile away now so keep
straight on, if you can, passing The Crown Inn on your right,
The Mitre Inn on your left and the Town Hall which stands at
the top of Gold Hill, the essential photographic subject of
any guide to England which is worth its salt. You start Day 5
by heading down Gold Hill so, for today, keep straight on into
the corner by King Alfred's Kitchen (more temptation).   There
is a black and gold pointer to "Abbey Ruins and Park Walk" so,
even though the lane is very narrow, you shouldn't be able to
miss it.   Out onto Park Walk, the wide promenade between the
Abbey walls and the gardens overlooking St James', the views
from the many benches are magnificent and, in company of many
chaffinches and blackbirds, let yourself wallow in the beauty
of the downs which are your next target now that you have
completely covered the Northern boundary of Cranborne Chase.

Shaftesbury was here long before the Normans arrived.   It is
listed as Sceptesberie, owned by the King, in the Domeseday
Book.

Whilst you sit here, let me tell you of some strange sightings
not far from your bench which were recorded by local residents
between the wars.   At the dissolution of the monasteries,
the last Abbess, Elizabeth Zouche, wanted to hide the great
treasure of the Convent of St Edward from the commissioners so
she "instructed one of the monks to bury it.   He did, but
dropped dead before he could reveal its whereabouts.   His
ghost is said to walk the Abbey grounds, vainly trying to tell
someone where he hid it amongst the ruins".   Perhaps he'll
tell you.   Anyway, ghostly monks are a common sight around
here.   Apparently, about 1905, "three monks with wide hats
were seen by an old inhabitant near St James Rectory" and, in
1920, "a monk with brown cowl and habit was seen to vanish
through a wall on the Old Abbey site".   Maybe it's time you
paid a visit to the ruins behind you - or to the Grosvenor
Hotel, the Ship Inn on Tout Hill or the Kings Arms in the Car
Park or Ye Old Two Brewers down in St James - not far from
the Rectory.   Or, perhaps, an early night with a good book
is called for.

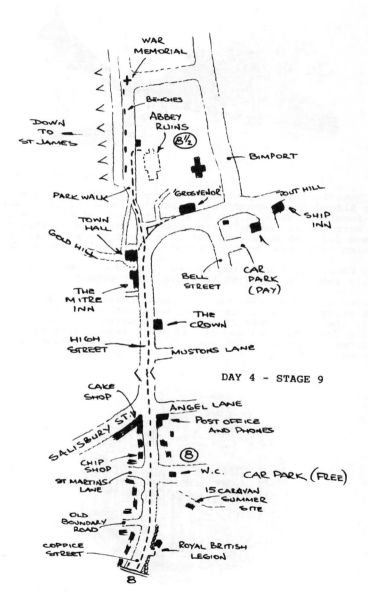

WAR MEMORIAL

DOWN TO ST JAMES

BENCHES

ABBEY RUINS

⑧½

BIMPORT

PARK WALK

'GROSVENOR'

TOUT HILL

SHIP INN

TOWN HALL

GOLD HILL

BELL STREET

CAR PARK (PAY)

THE MITRE INN

THE CROWN

HIGH STREET

MUSTONS LANE

DAY 4 - STAGE 9

CAKE SHOP

SALISBURY ST.

ANGEL LANE

POST OFFICE AND PHONES

⑧

CHIP SHOP

ST MARTINS LANE

W.C.

CAR PARK (FREE)

15 CARAVAN SUMMER SITE

OLD BOUNDARY ROAD

COPPICE STREET

ROYAL BRITISH LEGION

8

Park Walk. Page 106

The Benedictine Abbey of Shaftesbury was founded in 880 AD by King Alfred whose daughter, Aethelgiva, was its first Abbess. Its fame increased in 979 AD when the body of King Edward, who was martyred at Corfe Castle, was brought here.   This was the reason for Shaftesbury becoming a venue for pilgrims and many amazing cures have been recorded - all credited to St Edward.

King Canute died here but he was buried at Winchester, nearer to his famed tussle with the waves at Southampton.

Between 1080 and 1120, under Norman control, the Abbey and the town prospered but later rulers were not so benevolent and, in 1539, the last Abbess finally surrendered the Abbey to Henry VIII's Commissioners and it was demolished, much of the local glaucous sandstone being used to build fine residences within or near the town.

Shaftesbury's Monastic Seal

DAY 5 INTRODUCTION

Shaftesbury Abbey to Blandford Road A354

If you enjoyed the high country of Win Green on Day 4, today's downs and valleys will be especially exciting.   Leaving down Gold Hill, the required picture for every "Scenes of England" calender, you soon arrive at French Mill and Cann Mill in the valley before ascending Melbury Hill.   From here, the views into the deep valleys are brilliant and should be savoured - with a lake or two, you could be in the Lake District.

However, after a pleasant stroll down through West Wood and crossing Shepherds Bottom, a hauntingly good valley, you reach the highest village on Cranborne Chase - Ashmore, at 700 feet, with its ancient dew pond. The easy descent of Ashmore Bottom brings you to the land of great houses and old Chase families - but more of that and their ghosts later.

The grassy downs and the ancient woods provide pleasing, fresh air-filled walking today, so fill your lungs and stretch those legs - keeping your eyes open for deer, buzzards - and ghosts.

	STAGE	MILES	TOTAL
1	Shaftesbury Abbey to French Mill Lane	0.75	0.75
2	French Mill Lane to Mill Stream	0.75	1.50
3	Mill Stream to Melbury Abbas	0.75	2.25
4	Melbury Abbas to Melbury Down	0.75	3
5	Melbury Down to West Wood	1.25	4.25
6	West Wood to Ashmore	1	5.25
7	Ashmore to Well Bottom	1	6.25
8	Well Bottom to Ashmore Bottom	1	7.25
9	Ashmore Bottom to Stubhampton	1.25	8.50
10	Stubhampton to Eastbury Park	1	9.50
11	Eastbury Park to Chettle Long Barrow	1.25	10.75
12	Chettle Long Barrow to A354	1.25	12
CD	Chettle Diversion from Stage 12	1	[13]

You will need all three of the O S maps Nos 183, 184 and 195, but only the corners of any of them, since the Ordnance Survey don't seem to have been ready for "The Cranborne Chase Path". Wilts and Dorset buses Nos 139, X13 and 184 will take you to your start or finish for Day 5.

DAY 5 - STAGE 1

Shaftesbury Abbey to French Mill Lane

Leaving the Abbey, return to the top of Gold Hill.   This will
seem a familiar sight.   It's on practically every "Scenes of
England in Colour" calendar and is a superb starting point for
today's ramble.   Keeping to the buttressed stone wall on the
right, descend the railed, cobbled slope (tarmac at first) to
join the tarmac road surface as the slope reduces.   At the
T-junction with Layton Lane, "Ye Olde Two Brewers" is along to
your left but it's far too early.   Turn left and follow the
houses and hedged gardens around the bend, past Shooters Lane
on the way and, with a small field, a gate and a lay-by on the
left, the hillside drops away on your right.

Now uphill, after the bank of houses on your left, you come to
a cross-roads with a signpost on the corner showing "Salisbury
and Blandford" straight on up Hawkesdene Lane and "Manston and
Sturminster Newton" behind you.   Cross over and keep straight
up the hill, still with a hedged bank on your left and hedged
houses on your right.   Immediately after Boyne Mead on the
left, with a fenced footpath alongside it, turn off to your
right and go over the unsigned stile next to a farm gate. This
leads onto a high, level greensward.   After the house on your
left, the hedge borders fields for the first time today
whilst, on your right, the hillside drops down and is clothed
with beeches and oaks.   From here, you can look back towards
Gold Hill and see no less than four church towers on the side
and on top of Shaftesbury's ancient slopes.

Beyond the trees, you can see deep into the Stour Valley where
the River Stour flows steadily from Stourhead in Wiltshire all
the way to the sea at Christchurch in Dorset.   When you've
finished the Cranborne Chase Path, you will probably feel like
another rewarding challenge.   It's dispiriting when a long
planned and much enjoyed walk comes to an end and it's good to
have another aim in life.   So, make a note to get "The Stour
Valley Path" when you arrive in Wimborne.   Here endeth the
commercial.

Anyway, after a couple of gates in the hedge on your left, you
arrive at a stile next to a gate in the far corner.   There
are no Footpath arrows here to help but the path divides three
ways.   A path to your left goes into the top end of Cann
village, the one to your right takes you straight into French
Mill Lane and the one diagonally ahead leads to the stile in
the far RH corner of this field to bring you out further down
French Mill Lane.   Decisions, decisions.   So, in the lane,
turn left and begin to descend. Oh, and whilst in this shady,
sunken lane, let me regale you with a local story concerning a
three hundred years old barn which stood in Tree Ground, here
in French Mill Lane.   "Years ago, young people used to gather
in the old barn on Sundays to play cards.   But one Sunday, a
stranger appeared and offered to join in the game.   During
the course of play, he dropped a card and in stooping showed a
cloven hoof.   Result, no more Sunday gambling".

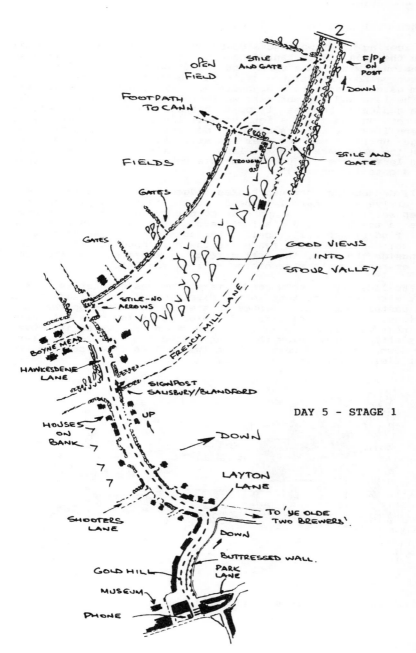

2

STILE AND GATE

OPEN FIELD

F/P ON POST

DOWN

FOOTPATH TO CANN

STILE AND GATE

FIELDS

TROUGH

GATES

GOOD VIEWS INTO STOUR VALLEY

GATES

STILE - NO ARROWS

FRENCH MILL LANE

BOYNE MEAD

HAWKESDENE LANE

SIGNPOST SALISBURY/BLANDFORD

DAY 5 - STAGE 1

HOUSES ON BANK

UP

DOWN

LAYTON LANE

SHOOTERS LANE

TO 'YE OLDE TWO BREWERS'

DOWN

BUTTRESSED WALL.

GOLD HILL

PARK LANE

MUSEUM

PHONE

DAY 5 - STAGE 2

French Mill Lane to Mill Stream

Considering that what goes down must come up again, carry on down the lane, with banked hedges on either side and with an occasional wire fence up on your left until, just before Spur House, a Footpath signed stile on the LH side, adjacent to a farm gate, leads into a high field. This path runs parallel to the lane and may not seem worth taking - but take it. The lane suddenly becomes trapped between high, steep banks - concrete on the right - for the next 100 yards and there is no escape if a car comes along. So follow the path behind the hedge until it emerges over the stile in the corner and comes down the bank back onto the lane. After this deep gulley, turn left at the T-junction with a cottage on the left corner and a gate facing you.

Still descending, between banked hedges and round a few bends, you arrive at a sharp left bend at the foot of a particularly steep section. Round this corner, with a Footpath-signed gate in the hedge and a selection of gates on the RH side, you will find French Mill itself. Facing the Mill, behind a gated and white-painted iron fence, is the mill pond whilst, running alongside the pond, the mill stream disappears under the lane and emerges by the side of the Mill on your right.

As the lane begins to ascend, take the unsigned stile in the left wire fence and keep to the direction of the stream across the pastureland which slopes up steeply to a farm on the high horizon. For the first 100 yards, stay low down but, when the next wire fence comes into view, turn up towards it. Over this stile, stay below the single tree and head for the far, low down, hedged LH corner where twin stiles take you into the next field, close to the stream.

Not French Mill. This is the next one, Cann Mill. Page 114

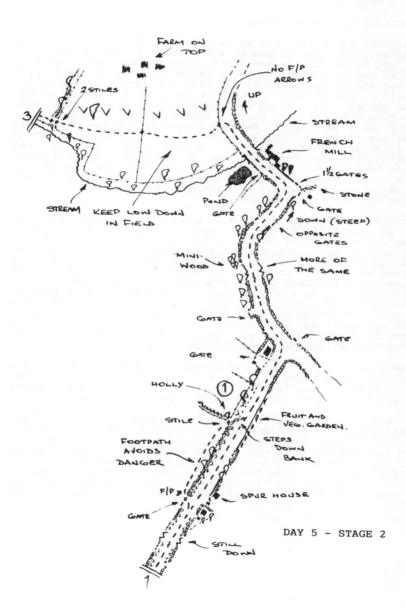

FARM ON TOP

2 STILES

3

STREAM

KEEP LOW DOWN IN FIELD

NO F/P ARROWS

UP

STREAM

FRENCH MILL

1½ GATES

STONE

POND GATE

GATE DOWN (STEEP)

OPPOSITE GATES

MORE OF THE SAME

MINI-WOOD

GATE

GATE

GATE

HOLLY

①

STILE

FRUIT AND VEG. GARDEN.

FOOTPATH AVOIDS DANGER

STEPS DOWN BANK

F/P

SPUR HOUSE

GATE

STILL DOWN

DAY 5 – STAGE 2

113

DAY 5 - STAGE 3

Mill Stream to Melbury Abbas

Immediately after the twin stiles, go over the stile in the LH
corner and cross the stream by the narrow, railed bridge. Turn
right and follow the fenced ditch, with the embankment on your
left, to the RH corner. Over the stile in the wire fence, pick
your way across the boggy field with the mass of marsh grass.
There is a modern house beyond the wood fence on your right.
In the corner, go through the steel gate onto the tarmac lane
which runs down into the yard on your right. A local, but
private, path runs uphill between hedges on the immediate left
whilst the large building with the Spanish looking windmill on
your right is Cann Mill. A mill on this site has been
producing flour for centuries and, at one time, provided flour
for the nuns of Shaftesbury Abbey - no wonder the lane was so
deep with all those deliveries being made. It must have been
the main haulage route from Cann Mill and French Mill up to
Shaftesbury for all those years.

Now continue along the lane, with a new row of trees along the
fence on your left and the mill pond down on your right, until
you arrive at the busy A350 Blandford to Shaftesbury road. A
great deal of care is needed here so, senses on full alert, go
across to the corner of Foots Hill opposite and hurry past the
bus stop and across the main road bridge. Don't stop until
you reach the pavement on the other side with the stone filled
gambions supporting the road edge. Immediately, drop down to
a stile with a Footpath arrow and cross the field to the twin
stiles in the fences which straddle a wide and boggy ditch. It
may be necessary for you to leap across this boggy patch from
a standing start, so make sure your cameras, binoculars, maps
and provisions are securely fastened.

In the next field, turn up the slope, on the top of which is a
fenced and gated house. You will find an exit stile in the
layered hedge in the far top left corner where a confirmation
Footpath post points back the way you have just come.

Turn left down the lane for a good few yards until, just after
a passing place, you arrive at the steep entrance to the car
park for "Melbury Abbas and Cann Village Hall". This perches
on an increasingly high embankment whilst, just opposite the
hall, a gate leads into a field and a stile takes its owner to
Rose Cottage. The hedged lane down on the left leads to
Barfoot Farm whilst you continue, between the hedge on your
left and the high bank on your right, downhill towards Melbury
Abbas.

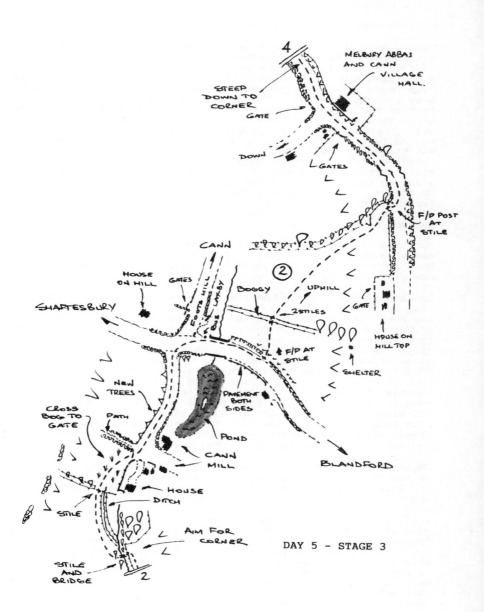

4

MELBURY ABBAS AND CANN VILLAGE HALL.

STEEP DOWN TO CORNER GATE

DOWN

GATES

F/P POST AT STILE

CANN

HOUSE ON HILL

GATES

② BOGGY

UPHILL

SHAFTESBURY

FOOTS MILL

BUS LAYBY

2 STILES

GATE

HOUSE ON HILL TOP

SHELTER

NEW TREES

F/P AT STILE

PAVEMENT BOTH SIDES

CROSS BOG TO GATE

PATH

POND

CANN MILL

BLANDFORD

STILE

HOUSE

DITCH

AIM FOR CORNER

DAY 5 - STAGE 3

STILE AND BRIDGE

2

115

DAY 5 - STAGE 4

Melbury Abbas to Melbury Down

You'll soon be up on the airy downs now, but there is a tricky
bit coming up next.   So, full concentration, please.   At the
foot of this hill, with a hedge on the LH bend, you will find
a Footpath signed stile next to a gate on your right.   This
gate leads into a steep-sided, scrub-laden valley which slopes
away to your right.   The tree and scrub-covered bank on the
left of the valley obscures our route from view but, do as the
arrow says and, around the tree which is immediately after the
stile, follow the LH sloping field which runs almost parallel
to the lane before these trees.   In the far RH corner which
was hidden by the rising ground,   you will find some steps cut
into the bank and with a helpful handrail to get you up to the
stile on the top. Again, follow the direction of the Footpath
arrow on the stile and cross the rising field towards its far
LH corner.   On the way, passing the tree-lined, meandering
fence along your left, you will find Manor Farm with its old,
stone barns beyond the wire fence with the gate in it at the
far end of your field.

Crossing this field, you will see the wooded slopes of Melbury
Beacon over on your right.   Our route takes us up to Melbury
Down but, on a more gentle rise, via the "saddle" between the
steep hill on your right and Compton Down on the left.

Go through the gate in the corner, with the Footpath signpost,
and turn left along the hedged and banked lane to arrive at
the many fine, stone buildings of Manor Farm, with a good view
of Melbury Abbas church ahead of you.   As the hedge gives way
to wire fence on the right, go straight past the gate into the
first field but turn right through the kissing gate into the
second field.   This should be a kissing gate by the time of
your arrival as the thoughtful, farming gentleman from Manor
Farm intends to install such a gate for the benefit of those
who have trouble with climbing over stiles. Such consideration
deserves our thanks.   Now, through the gate, closely follow
the wire fence, past a trough and a gate, all the way up this
wide open field.   On the way, the fence becomes elevated on a
grassy ridge for a while near the top.   Whether these are
ancient or more modern earthworks, I cannot tell you.

Through the narrow, woodland strip which runs along the slopes
of the hill, go through the half-gate onto the steep hillside
of "Melbury Hill", a unique chalk upland grazing area which is
under the protection of the National Trust.

After this short, but steep ascent, have a breather before you
head straight up the slopes facing you.   On the way to the top
fence, you are joined by a green track which comes, twisting
and turning, up from your left.   This will lead you, still
straight on, through the ancient, long dykes of Melbury Hill,
to another half-gate where you may be allowed to lean for a
while and regain your breath again.   Don't go through this
gate but turn left and follow the fence up towards the top of
Compton Down, admiring the superb views all round.

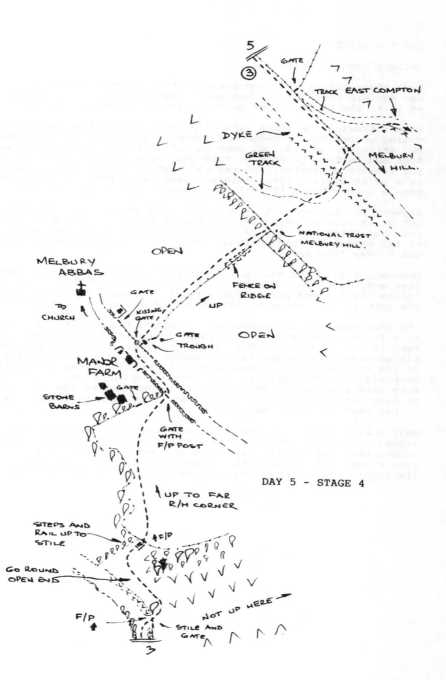

DAY 5 - STAGE 4

DAY 5 - STAGE 5

Melbury Down to West Wood

From these slopes and from several other viewpoints today, you
can see Win Green on the horizon.   Not surprizing, I suppose,
as it is the highest spot on the whole of Cranborne Chase.

Keep following the fence, now with the 1 in 6 Spreadeagle Hill
coming up behind the hedge and fence on your left, to the gate
and stile at the end. Go over the stile by the National Trust
sign and follow the edge of this busy road for 200 yards until
you reach the sanctuary of the car park on your right.   There
is a safer field, with a gate at either end, but this does not
have a path through it so I can't advise you to go that way.

Anyway, in the car park, you will find several marked routes
out of it, two of which lead to East Compton.   Incidentally,
you can catch the X13 or 139 bus to Blandford or Shaftesbury
at the church in Compton Abbas about 1.1/2 miles straight down
the By-Way from here.

However, follow the National Trust marked path parallel to the
road and, at the end of the fence, go over the stile.   Don't
follow the arrowed path to your right, but go straight through
the gate in the corner by the woods and out onto the road.

The road opposite is signposted   "Compton Abbas Airfield" and
this is the route you have to take.   Carefully cross over and
keep to the RH edge of this road.   There are a few parking
places along the verges in the woods on your right at first.
As you walk along this roadside, the woods on your right are
deep and have the familiar bank just along the edge.   It's
much more interesting on your left, though, where the airfield
is busy with small aircraft constantly buzzing in and out, as
it has been for many, many years.

Half a mile along this road, a track turns off into the woods,
signed "Forestry Commission, West Wood".   Turn in here and go
around the edge of the gate onto the main, stony track which
runs slightly downhill with a tree-lined fence on its left. On
its right, the woods are mainly beeches and full of bird song.

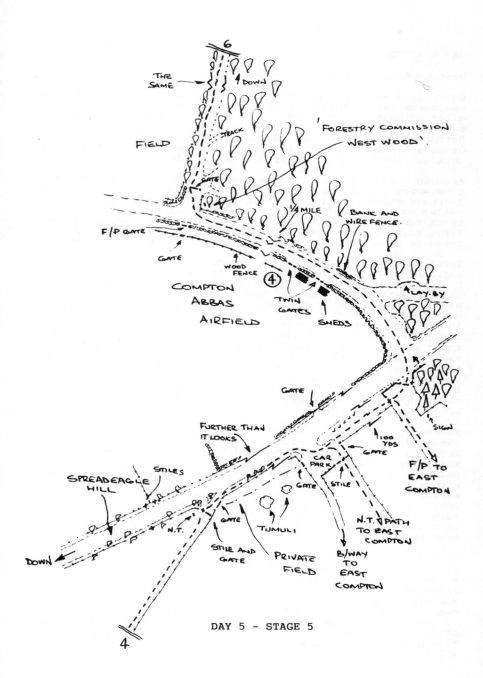

6

THE SAME

DOWN

FIELD

TRACK

'FORESTRY COMMISSION WEST WOOD'.

GATE

¼ MILE

BANK AND WIRE FENCE.

F/P GATE

GATE

WOOD FENCE

④

COMPTON ABBAS AIRFIELD

TWIN GATES

SHEDS

A LAY-BY

GATE

FURTHER THAN IT LOOKS

SIGN

STILES

100 YDS

GATE

SPREADEAGLE HILL

CAR PARK

F/P TO EAST COMPTON

GATE

STILE

N.T.

GATE

TUMULI

N.T. & PATH TO EAST COMPTON

DOWN

STILE AND GATE

PRIVATE FIELD

B/WAY TO EAST COMPTON

DAY 5 - STAGE 5

4

DAY 5 - STAGE 6

West Wood to Ashmore

Carry on down the woodland track - where I was fortunate to
see a roe deer turning off from the path in front of me - and,
after an open area of gates and fences when the woods end, you
emerge onto an open field which drops away into Shepherds
Bottom ahead of you. Follow the green track alongside the LH
hedge and fence, past a trough in the hedge, and through the
next gate with fenced hedges on either side.

Keep to the descending track across the open field to the next
gate which crosses your path. Through this gate, the track
descends steeply, with a bank on your left and a drop into the
valley on your right. At the bottom of the track, another
track runs along the near edge of a mixed wood towards Washers
Pit - a mysterious spot which is right on the edge of a huge
forested area but which was formerly deep within the forest.

Until the mid-1800's, when the Ashmore to Fontmell track was
upgraded to a firm road, a Bronze Age bowl barrow (No. 3e in
L V Grinsell's "Barrows of Dorset"), stood at Washers Pit but
it was destroyed by the new road. Until that time, strange,
airborne noises and a rattling of chains had haunted this spot
but the destruction of the barrow and the removal of the bones
to Ashmore churchyard appears to have calmed the spirits and
brought an end to the noises. Also at this spot, a woman was
found hanging by her hair from an ash tree overhanging the now
vanished well. She was cut down by a rescuer who was moved by
three dreams to visit the spot. And, to disquiet you still
further, a woman in white is said to brush against travellers
in the dark between Washers Pit and Spinney's Pond. I don't
think any of these happenings are considered to come this far
up the valley though.

However, think no more about it and skirt around the LH end of
the wood, with a "No Right of Way" gate on your left, and
begin to climb out of Shepherds Bottom, passing a stile into
the woods, and up to the first gate which crosses your path
between the LH fence and the RH wood. Walk up the green track
with a wire fence on your left to the next gate with a steep
bank now on your right. Continuing upwards, the track becomes
less clear as you approach the next gate, with deep mud after
rain or bumps and hollows at other times. On the left, there
is a notice intending to banish all wheeled vehicles from this
Bridleway.

With a row of ivy-clad trees on the right, go through the next
gate to a slightly sunken track with grass up the middle, with
a hedge to the left and a fence to the right. Keep to the
track as it begins to level out beyond the hedge on the left.
Now with fences on both sides, keep on past all of the gates,
past the "ski-jump" on the right and over the mud-laden track
to the exit onto the Ashmore road. The farm on your left
is Manor Farm and now, with a fenced field facing you and the
road going down to Washers Pit on your right, turn left to the
village. You could always come back to Washers Pit tonight.

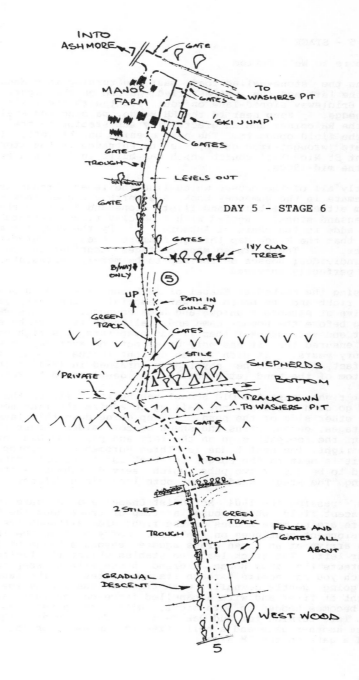

INTO ASHMORE

GATE

MANOR FARM

GATES

TO WASHERS PIT

'SKI JUMP'

GATES

TROUGH

GATE

LEVELS OUT

GATE

DAY 5 – STAGE 6

GATES

IVY CLAD TREES

B/WAY ONLY

⑤

UP

PATH IN GULLEY

GREEN TRACK

GATES

STILE

'PRIVATE'

SHEPHERDS BOTTOM

TRACK DOWN TO WASHERS PIT

GATE

DOWN

2 STILES

TROUGH

GREEN TRACK

FENCES AND GATES ALL ABOUT

GRADUAL DESCENT

WEST WOOD

5

DAY 5 - STAGE 7

Ashmore to Well Bottom

Along the stone-walled road, past the turning into Manor Farm
on the left and the white-railed garden on the right, ignore
the Bridleway signed lane on your right with the stile in its
LH hedge.   Keep near to the RH verge, passing the small wood
on the RH corner and an electricity sub-station in the corner
of the field opposite.   The next opening on the left, with the
ornate wrought-iron gates, is the entrance to the stone   and
flint St Nicholas' church which was built in 1423 and restored
in the mid-1900s.

Nearly all of the houses which line the lanes through Ashmore,
Aisemare in the Domesday Book, are worth a closer look - built
from either fine brick and flint, stone and flint or the local
greensand stone.   Roofed with fine clay tiles or thatch, each
one adds to the charm of Ashmore.   By the way, let me just
say that the Stage Map through Ashmore does not purport to be
exact.   There are so many cottages, consider the positions
of individual houses on the map to be merely representational,
not perfectly surveyed.

Passing the Methodist Chapel of 1855 and the Old Parsonage on
the right and the bench and war memorial on the left, you will
arrive at Ashmore's unique and huge dewpond.   This was here
long before the Romans came and, although it works by storing
mist and rain quicker than it can evaporate, its high position
has ensured that it has only dried out, on average, once every
twenty years.   It didn't even dry out in the drought of 1976.
In fact, it had to be physically drained in 1994 so that the
bottom of the pond (at about 16 feet deep) could be resealed.

Bear right, past the Old School behind its rails on the corner
and go down the lane, not failing to admire the fine houses on
the other side of the pond.   Keep going down this lane, past
cottages, gates, barns and sheds on both sides, past the lane
with the Footpath sign on the left and past the Old Forge on
the right. The next house is "Three Horseshoes", appropriately
as it is next to the Forge, but that isn't the only reason. It
used to be one of two pubs which served Ashmore - the other
being "The Stag's Head" - but both long since defunct.

Now, passing the 1904 Methodist Chapel and the gate into the
adjacent field which houses a clump of trees near the Chapel,
there are no more houses on the right side although the ribbon
development continues on the left. Carry on down the lane and
you arrive at an open grass square beyond a hedge of firs on
your left. The track leads to stables whilst the facing hedge
protects the Manor House, a grand house with a sweeping drive
which you can admire through its open gates.   The lane keeps
on going, gently downhill, with trees in the wide verge on the
right at first and with a panelled fence on the left, and then
it becomes hedged on both sides, with a few gates, as far as
the left turning for Mud Oak Farm.   Carry on down the lane,
past another gate and a holly tree in the hedge on the RH side
and a gate on the LH side.

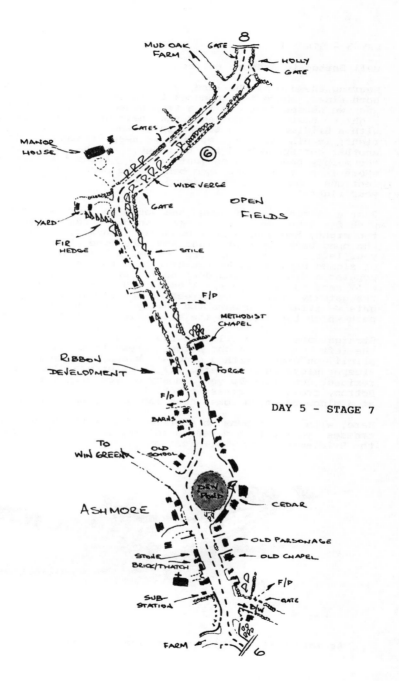

MUD OAK FARM
GATE
8
HOLLY GATE
GATES
MANOR HOUSE
6
WIDE VERGE
OPEN FIELDS
GATE
YARD
FIR HEDGE
STILE
F/P
METHODIST CHAPEL
RIBBON DEVELOPMENT
FORGE
F/P
DAY 5 - STAGE 7
BARNS
TO WIN GREEN
OLD SCHOOL
ASHMORE
DEW POND
CEDAR
OLD PARSONAGE
OLD CHAPEL
STONE BRICK/THATCH
F/P
GATE
SUB STATION
B/W
FARM
6

DAY 5 - STAGE 8

Well Bottom to Ashmore Bottom

Nearing the end of the lane, with no verges but with hedges on
both sides, there is a paddock field and stabling on your left
and two houses nestling in a tree-bedecked hollow down on the
right. Past these cottages and their entrance gates, a track
with a Bridleway arrow turns uphill and through a gate on your
right, leading into a deep wood. Keep straight on down, past
another cottage behind the LH hedge, on the grassy track with
the mainly beech wood on your right. After the last cottage,
there is a small, new wood behind the hedge whilst the woods
continue - harvested, replanted, open and full of bird song on
your right.

Just a little further down, the woods on your left are planted
with fir trees and, if you peer into the depths, you will see
two mighty Redwoods - most unusual. Anyway, after bracken on
the open banks on your right and the pine strip continuing on
your left, a section of coppiced hazel leads you to a junction
of signed Bridleways at the exit from the woods. This is a
popular riding area and deep hoofprints are everywhere, so you
will need to watch your ankles as you walk. However, through
the gateway, follow the direction of a Bridleway arrow on the
gate - straight on down the valley - not up the very obvious
path which turns off up the steep slope to your left.

Straight ahead, you will see two trees with a definite lean to
the left. Go straight between these trees and enjoy an easy
stroll, on grass, with a gradual slope up to your right and a
steeper slope on your left. All is quiet grassland, with a few
resident cows to keep you company as you progress down Ashmore
Bottom, crossing a grassy track from left to right, to arrive
at a pinewood which comes down the bank from your right.

Here, with cattle pens on your left, go through the gate which
crosses your path and keep strolling down in the direction of
the Bridleway arrow - straight on.

Ashmore Bottom. (Between the leaning trees). This Page

124

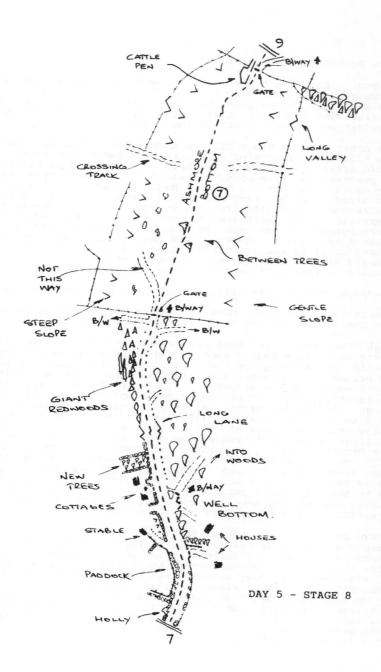

CATTLE PEN

9

B/WAY

GATE

LONG VALLEY

CROSSING TRACK

ASHMORE BOTTOM

(7)

BETWEEN TREES

NOT THIS WAY

GATE
B/WAY

GENTLE SLOPE

STEEP SLOPE

B/W

B/W

A A
A A
A

GIANT REDWOODS

LONG LANE

INTO WOODS

NEW TREES

B/WAY

WELL BOTTOM.

COTTAGES

STABLE

HOUSES

PADDOCK

DAY 5 - STAGE 8

HOLLY

7

125

DAY 5 - STAGE 9

Ashmore Bottom to Stubhampton

Up on your right, the track leads to Ashmore Barn Farm whilst the high ground on your left is Manor Hill. Keep on down the valley bottom to the gate in the next wire fence and, on the other side, you join a track with grass up the middle, a hedge on the left and an open field on the right.

On the other side of Manor Hill is Bussey Stool Farm and some of the tracks and fields of this farm bear names that recall a terrible affray which took place here in December 1780 between seven poachers and five Chase keepers. In the battle, the leader of the poachers, a Trumpet Major blessed with the name of Blandford, had his hand severed by a keepers blade and one of the keepers later died from his wounds but, in deference to the terrible wounds which they had suffered, the poachers were not transported, as was usual for such offences, but they were imprisoned instead. Superstition has it that bodies should be buried complete but Blandford's hand was buried in Pimperne churchyard after the affray and, years later, when he died and was buried in London, it was not reunited with his body.

Sure enough, the hand is still around, searching for its body.

The parts of Bussey Stool Farm to which I refer are known as Bloody Shard Gate, Bloody Field and Bloodway Coppice.

Through the gate in the next wooden fence, the track becomes concrete as it goes past a modern, red-brick house on the left and a wide grassy verge on the right. The hill is still steep beyond the house but the right hand slope becomes a lot less pronounced as you progress. Through the gate after the concrete track, there is an open hazel coppice on the left and a fenced field on the right. After an opening into this field and a gate into the next, follow the flint and grass track past the clipped hedge of 'Holmes Lea' and, after the last cob cottage on the left, you emerge onto the Tarrant Hinton to Iwerne Minster road. Where the road turns away to your right, turn to the left and enjoy an easy stroll along the cottage-lined road through Stubhampton, Stibemetune in the Domesday Book. There are some fine flint, brick and stone barns to see along this road, one of which holds a post box in its wall, but you may need to tack along the road to make sure the traffic can see you around the slight bends.

You have only just left the valley floor of Ashmore Bottom but you are now in another valley. This is an extension of Stubhampton Bottom, the furthest point of the Tarrant Valley and the source of the River Tarrant which gives its name to so many villages on its way to join the Stour between Wimborne and Blandford. Now, along the lane, you pass a complex of gates on your right which includes two stiles. These are both private, so keep going down the road for a while longer, past some flint and brick barns, some corrugated iron barns, hedges on both sides, a holly tree on the left and a house on the right - in that order.

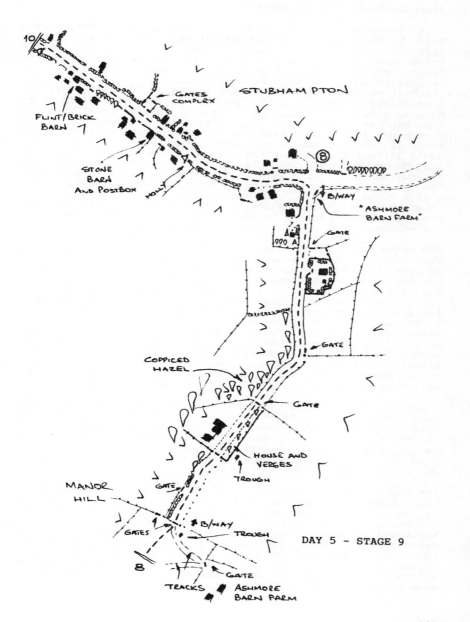

10//

STUBHAMPTON

GATES COMPLEX

FLINT/BRICK BARN

STONE BARN AND POSTBOX

HOLLY

B/WAY

"ASHMORE BARN FARM"

GATE

GATE

COPPICED HAZEL

GATE

HOUSE AND VERGES

TROUGH

MANOR HILL

GATE

GATES

B/WAY

TROUGH

DAY 5 - STAGE 9

8

GATE

TRACKS

ASHMORE BARN FARM

127

DAY 5 - STAGE 10

Stubhampton to Eastbury Park

In a few yards, after a Water Board enclosure and the chicken sheds on the right, turn up the next RH track with a Bridleway post and, after about 30 yards, turn up the bank on the left and go over the stile with the Footpath arrow pointing up the field, parallel with the road. The bridleway itself carries on up to Harbin's Park, the scene of a well documented argument between rival landowners in 1749. Gunville Park was then owned by Squire Harbin whilst George Pitt, later Lord Rivers, owned nearby Rushmore Lodge, nr Tollard Royal (not far from Win Green on Day 4). Pitt's keepers complained that Harbin was luring deer from the Chase into his park by laying out pulp from the apples left over after cider making. The smell attracted the deer from miles around and, once they had leaped over Harbin's fence to get at the pulp, they could not get out again. Pitt ordered one of his keepers to pull down the fence and to force the gates but they didn't find any deer within Harbin's Park. The ensuing case at Dorchester Assizes in which Harbin sued John Bailey, the keeper, for trespass and criminal damage appears to have been settled out of Court and the embanked wood bears Harbin's name to this day.

Now, with the wire fence on your left and the open field up on your right, ascend the grassy path to the top of the hill and go down the other side. The village of Stubhampton stretches out below but I'm not exactly certain where it becomes Tarrant Gunville. Keeping in a straight line, climb over the next stile, by the strip of pine wood on your right, into the next field and, with a hedge on the left and more woods over on the right, keep on to climb over another stile ahead of you in the wire fence. Over this field, passing two LH gates on the way, go over yet another stile next to some trees and drop down the bank on the other side where a gate lurks below on your left. Finally, bear right in this last field, not towards the gate in the RH hedge but aiming for the far right corner where you will find an exit stile with a Footpath arrow on its far side.

Cross over the hedged road and pass through the kissing gate onto a short path which leads to St Mary's, Tarrant Gunville. This stone and flint church, with its typically squat tower, was built in 1503 but it was heavily restored in 1845 when all congregations were increasing nationally. Inside there is a memorial to Thomas Wedgwood, son of the more famous Josiah Wedgwood, potter of Etruria, Staffs.

Leaving past a viburnum bush and going down the steps between high stone walls, go round the LH corner with The Old Rectory on your right and you arrive back at the road with a car park for about five cars next to a small wood on the left. Turn right and go down to the T-junction, with cottages across the Tarrant stream which faces you. A road sign shows distances to Salisbury and Shaftesbury. Turn right and, after Little Tarrant on the LH corner, turn left into School Lane with the railings of Eastbury Park on your right. There is something I have to tell you about Eastbury, but not until you are alone.

128

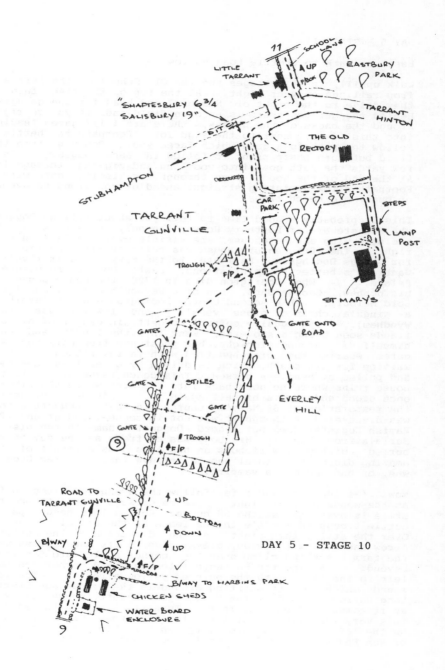

11

SCHOOL LANE

↑UP

P/BOX

LITTLE TARRANT

EASTBURY PARK

"SHAPTESBURY 6¾
SALISBURY 19"

DITCH

TARRANT HINTON

THE OLD RECTORY

STUBHAMPTON

CAR PARK

STEPS

TARRANT
GUNVILLE

LAMP POST

TROUGH

F/P

St MARY'S

GATES

GATE ONTO ROAD

GATE

STILES

GATE

EVERLEY HILL

GATE

⑨

TROUGH

F/P

ROAD TO
TARRANT GUNVILLE

↑UP

BOTTOM

DAY 5 - STAGE 10

↑DOWN

B/WAY

↑UP

F/P

B/WAY TO HARBINS PARK

CHICKEN SHEDS

WATER BOARD ENCLOSURE

9

DAY 5 - STAGE 11

Eastbury Park to Chettle Long Barrow

Walk uphill, past cottages and the Old School on the left and
iron railings on your right. At the top of the rise, turn up
the drive to the right of Number 7 and head for the garages.
Behind the garages there is an open field and, as you go right
around the backs of the houses, there are 1.1/2 gates leading
into this field, next to the sign for "Footpath to Chettle".
Follow the path to a gate which faces you. Don't go into the
field but turn sharp right to follow the back hedges. In a
few yards the path goes into woodland and zig-zags through it.
At the end of the wood, pass through the kissing gate with a
Footpath arrow pointing straight ahead of you along an avenue
of huge, old beech trees.

This is probably a good time to tell you about William Doggett
who was steward of Eastbury House, the only remnants of which,
a single wing and gatehouse, are visible over the Park on your
right. The 18th Century house was built by Sir John Vanbrugh
for George Dodington, Paymaster to the Navy, and it rivalled
Vanbrugh's better known creations, Castle Howard and Blenheim
Palace. When Dodington died in 1720, the house passed to
his nephew, George Bubb, son of a Weymouth chemist and later
Lord Melbury. This second George Dodington's diary "exhibits
a singular chain of gross venality and low intrigue" (H P
Wyndham). The equally corrupt Doggett, in danger of his own
frauds soon being discovered, went into the library and shot
himself. Around midnight, his ghost now frequents the Park
gates, wearing knee breeches tied with yellow ribbon. He is
waiting for his coach, which is driven by a headless coachman
and pulled by headless horses. This coach takes him up to the
house ruins where he goes back into the area where the library
once stood and shoots himself again. Apparently, during
the restoration of St Mary's church in 1845, Doggett's tomb
was discovered, although it was not in consecrated ground (The
Parish Register does not record Doggett's name in the List of
Burials from 1720). His body was as fresh as the day he was
buried - with yellow ribbons on his legs. As a result of this
amazing discovery, local people believe that William Doggett
was, or had become, a vampire.

Now, feeling warm and safe, follow the avenue of trees as far
as the woods on your right. A fence crosses your path and the
stile is over against the LH hedge. Follow this hedge, past a
cattle trough to a stile in the fence at the end of the hedge.
Over the stile, turn right, in the direction of the Footpath
arrow and follow the wide, grassy ride to its end. Cross over
the farm track and climb over the corner stile into the field
beyond. Follow the RH hedge into the field corner and bear
left to the stile with the painted yellow arrow. The long
mound which you are skirting around is the Bronze Age Chettle
Long Barrow. Over the stile, join a soft, rough bridleway
as it comes up from your left. Turn right, along the edge of
this very long field until the track narrows next to the wood
on the left, plunging into overgrown brambles and bushes with
broken Eastbury Park railings in the bushes on your right.

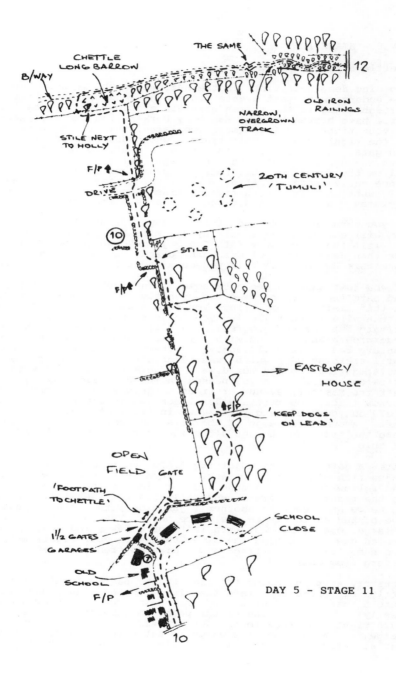

THE SAME

CHETTLE
LONG BARROW

B/WAY

OLD IRON
RAILINGS

12

NARROW,
OVERGROWN
TRACK

STILE NEXT
TO HOLLY

F/P

DRIVE

20TH CENTURY
'TUMULI'.

10

STILE

F/P

EASTBURY
HOUSE

F/P

'KEEP DOGS
ON LEAD'

OPEN
FIELD   GATE

'FOOTPATH
TO CHETTLE'

SCHOOL
CLOSE

1½ GATES
GARAGES

OLD
SCHOOL
F/P

DAY 5 - STAGE 11

10

DAY 5 - STAGE 12

Chettle Long Barrow to A354

Avoiding deep hoofprints in the narrower path, keep on through
the undergrowth, past a gate into the woods on your left and
through a gap in the broken wire fence across your track. You
still have broken bits of Eastbury Park's iron fence appearing
on your right. After a more open area, this fence turns away
to the right and the main track, which has been wider since
the gate, turns left into the woods. Don't follow it. Turn
down the narrower path to the right of the main track and
follow the forest of Christmas trees on your left, with a wire
fence on its edge. After several yards, the path arrives at
a T-junction with another large track and you have to make a
decision - not a difficult one if you're already tired.

If you turn left here and follow Map CD (Chettle Diversion),
you will extend today's walk by one mile but you will be going
to visit the fine Early 18th Century house which was built for
the then Head Ranger of Cranborne Chase, George Chafin. If you
take this Route, I'll tell you more about it when you arrive.

If you just want to get back home, turn right through the gate
and onto the track between two open fields. A long, easy walk
on this rising By-way brings you to a mixed wood on the right,
with a wire fence following you on your left. This wood is
private but, as you progress, you will see, hidden in the deep
undergrowth and covered with ivy, many small sections of 20th
Century red brick buildings. These are remains of a World
War 1 training camp which was reinstated, on a more permanent
basis, during the 2nd World War, as were the "tumuli" with the
brick entrances which you passed in the RH field after you had
left the Eastbury avenue of trees. Anyway, at the end of the
narrow track, you meet a wider track which comes out from the
field on your left and turns down in front of you. Turn
left, around the edge of the gate and past the silage tank,
onto the track which runs alongside the bushes on the RH edge
of this field.

After a gate into the adjoining field, your route arrives at a
T-junction with another track. Turn left towards some barns
and follow the track around the far side of the barns, bearing
to the right. The track bends a little but keep following the
RH hedge and fence to another T-junction with a slurry pond in
the banked enclosure on its LH corner. The RH turn goes into
a large, open field but turn left for a few yards and, with a
fenced new wood behind the older bushes on your right, keep on
the same track. (The track now coming up from your left is the
return from Chettle).

However, keep following the same track, past a turning between
strips of fenced wood into the field on the right, and plunge
into a narrow, overgrown and descending path (the Bridleway,
really). At the end of the path, you emerge onto the A354.
Turn right and cross to the other side for the firmer grass
verge. Walk along the verge to catch your bus or find your
car at Tarrant Hinton, just 1/2 mile away down the hill.

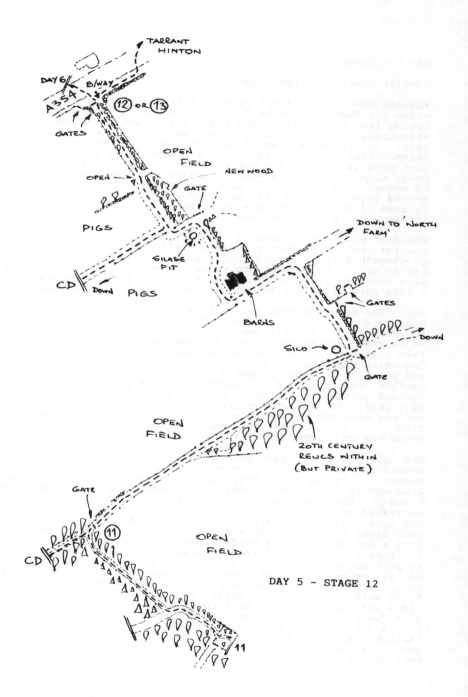

DAY 5 - STAGE 12

DAY 5 - STAGE CD

Chettle Diversion from Stage 12

Turning down the LH track, you will find it narrower for a few
yards but then it emerges from the trees to join a wider track
coming from your left. Bear right and follow the wider track,
with trees on the right and the remnants of the wood on your
left, to a farm gate and a personnel gate - with not an arrow
between them but which lead into a grassy field with old trees
scattered about.   Aim for the gate in the wire fence at the
other side of the field where a grassy track goes off into the
LH corner to join another, more used track.   Through this
second gate, you come into parkland which is the domain of the
Caravan Club.   If you manage to look exhausted (and you most
likely are), you may be able to scrounge a cup of tea.

Ahead of you, the RH edge of Chettle House comes into view but
aim for the far LH corner of this field, towards a gate. Don't
go through this gate but turn right about 20 yards before you
get to it.   Go between the wooden fence on your left and the
wire fence on your right.   In the dip ahead of you, there is
a farm gate, slightly to the left and next to a small wood.

Over the fence on your left, there is a fine view of Chettle
House and part of the lovely gardens which open to visitors in
the summer.   Chettle House was built for George Chafin when
he married Sir Anthony Sturt's daughter and they lived here
from 1710 onwards.   George was Head Ranger for the whole of
Cranborne Chase as was his father before him.   This fine,
red-brick house was probably the work of the designer of
Smith's Square Church in London as both exhibit the unusual
rounded corners.   The house took 25 years to complete.   The
last Chafin to live at Chettle House was William, born in 1732
and the eleventh of George's sons, of whom seven had already
died.   William was the locally famous author of "Notes and
Anecdotes of Cranborne Chase", who died in 1818.

Now, go through the gate by the wood and into a lowering field
beyond it. There is a vineyard on your right, South facing of
course.   Follow the grassy track, with wire fences on either
side uphill to the next gate.   Through the gate, there are
trees in the track on your left and Thickthorn Long Barrow,
excavated in 1700, on top of the hill on your right.   Through
the gate next to the barrow, follow the LH hedge to where the
path dives into some bushes ahead of you.   In here, you will
find a half gate with a Bridleway arrow. Before going through
it, take time to look directly ahead across the field and try
to pick out a red Gas Pipe post on the far side. If you can't
see it, no matter.   The route heads straight across from here
but, if the field is overgrown, follow the hedge around to the
right until, you reach a stile near the Gas Pipe post which
leads into a narrow open section, between woods.   Do not go
over the stile into this narrow wood area but keep straight on
to its end, where a main track comes from your left and goes
through the strip of woodland on your right.   Turn right, onto
the track, and follow it uphill, across open fields, until you
meet up again with Stage 12.

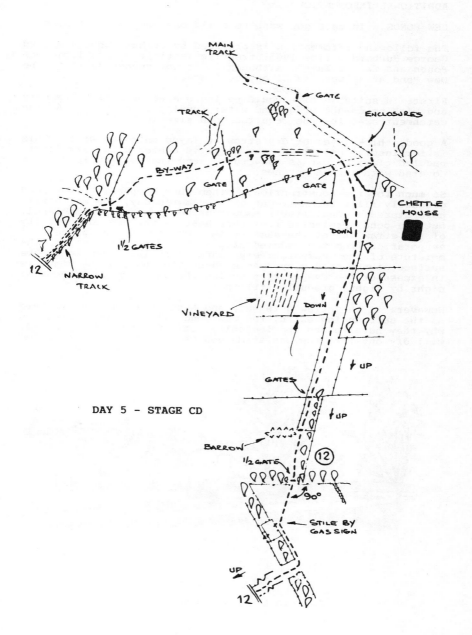

MAIN TRACK

GATE

ENCLOSURES

TRACK

BY-WAY

GATE

GATE

CHETTLE HOUSE

DOWN

1½ GATES

12

NARROW TRACK

VINEYARD

DOWN

UP

GATES

DAY 5 - STAGE CD

UP

BARROW

(12)

½ GATE

90°

STILE BY GAS SIGN

UP

12

ADDITIONAL INFORMATION

DEW PONDS - In case you want to build one when you get home.

The following information is provided by Arthur Hubbard's and George Hubbard's fine 1905 treatise entitled "Neolithic Dew Ponds and Cattle Ways", although it is not suggested that the Dew Pond at Ashmore is of any such age.

First, a suitable site would be in an area with high humidity and with no chance of ground water running into it. A wide catchment area for the required pond size is best.

A good, thick layer of dry straw is layed onto the soil. This is for insulation. Then, the straw is coated with very finely puddled clay, known as the crust, and the surface is finally covered with rounded stones.

So much for the construction. Then what happens? The pond gradually fills because, during a summer's day, the earth will have stored a considerable amount of heat - (Yes, in England), but the pond, protected from this heat by the non-conductivity of the straw is, at the same time, chilled by the process of evaporation from the puddled clay. So, during the night, the moisture of the comparatively warm air is condensed on the surface of the cold clay. As condensation during the night is in excess of the evaporation during the day, the pond becomes, night by night, gradually filled.

However, if the straw gets wet, and hence the same temperature as the surrounding earth, the dew pond will not work. That is why they have to be periodically relaid and, if neglected, will dry out like the one at Maiden Castle Fort, Dorchester.

Ashmore Dew Pond. Page 122

DAY 6 INTRODUCTION

Blandford Road A354 to Wimborne Minster

The high downs and deep valleys of Day 5 were really dramatic and, although much of today will again be spent at high level, with magnificent views, the walking is easier as the hills are less steep . The scenery is far more tranquil and the vast panorama is more the verdant patchwork of pasture and farming country rather than the steep coombes and hills of yesterday.

This last Day takes you along farm tracks, through forests and across fruitful fields to Badbury Rings from where spreads the vast network of Roman roads which crosses Cranborne Chase and continues far beyond its boundaries.

From Badbury Rings, our route follows the boundary of Kingston Lacy house, glimpses of which are obtained through the trees in its parkland because so many of its magnificent trees were lost in the fierce gales of 1987 and 1990.

Finally, after enjoying much of the Kingston Lacy Estate, now in the ownership of the National Trust, you return to Wimborne Minster and reward yourself with that well earned pint or that cream tea which you promised yourself on Day 1 when you walked away from the Minster and first set foot on "The Cranborne Chase Path"

STAGE		MILES	TOTAL
1	A354 to Launceston Down	1	1
2	Launceston Down to Little Down	1	2
3	Little Down to Dean Hill Coppice	1.25	3.25
4	Dean Hill Coppice to Hemsworth Farm	1	4.25
5	Hemsworth Farm to Bradford Path	1	5.25
6	Bradford Path to Badbury Rings	1.25	6.50
7	Badbury Rings to B3082	0.75	7.25
8	B3082 to Kingston Lacy Park	1.50	8.75
9	Kingston Lacy Park to Pamphill	0.75	9.50
10	Pamphill to River Stour	1	10.50
11	River Stour to Wimborne Minster	0.75	11.25

For this final Day, O S map No 195 covers the whole route and Wilts and Dorset buses Nos X13 and 184 serve start and finish, so there isn't much excess baggage to carry today.

DAY 6 - STAGE 1

A354 to Launceston Down

At the start of a really superb Day's walk, return to the Toll
House on the A354 and the first puzzle of the day.   What do
the letters Pd Ct Tg and the date 1827 mean on the wall of the
Toll House?   According to Ronald Good in "The Old Roads of
Dorset 1940, this Toll House wasn't built until 1833.   Now,
just to the left of the Toll House, turn through the farm gate
with a signpost which proclaims "Bridleway Manswood 3 and Dean
Farm 3.3/4".   On the grassy verge of this vast field, follow
the garden fence and hedge around to the corner, then follow
the hedge up to the first gate in the wire fence on the right.
Go through the gate where a faint blue arrow points into this
field and you need to follow the fence, now on the left, which
leads you to the corner and up the field slope to your right.
Already, you have fine views down to your left but you can see
almost forever from the top of this field.   At the gate next
to the water tank, go through and linger awhile.   If it's
windy, you can listen to the whistling from the "flute" hole
in the gatepost and, turning round, you can see Win Green from
Day 4 immediately above the Toll House and Ashmore from Day 5
above the tops of some barns to the left.

Turn round again and cross this next, open field to the gate
posts opposite.   Stop again and, looking around, you will be
able to pick out, in clockwise order starting with the line of
the fence on your left, Blandford Army Camp tower, Hambledon
Hill, Tarrant Hinton, Tarrant Gunville and Ashmore.   However,
it's time to get going - no more lingering for a while.   Past
the mixed wood on your left, follow the fenced-in and grassy
track for about 1/4 mile, passing a low tumulus on your right
on the way.

You are now joined by a new plantation of young beeches on the
right - Hyde Hill Plantation, which stretches for another 1/4
mile until you arrive at a gate across your track.   Through
the gate, you come onto a wide, squarish, grassy area which
leads you by way of rutted tracks to the far LH corner and
back onto a continuation of our route, albeit more rutted than
the earlier part and with an accompanying hedge on the right.
In yet another 1/4 mile, a track turns down to your right but
it only leads into fields.   Keep straight on, through the
facing gate with another blue painted arrow on it, back onto a
rutted track with grass up the middle.   At first, there is
a mixed wood on the left with a track turning into it but keep
to our Bridleway.

..the fenced-in, grassy path. This Page

138

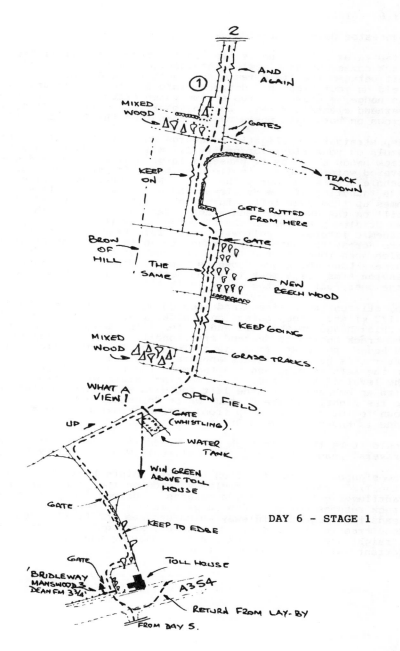

DAY 6 - STAGE 1

139

DAY 6 - STAGE 2

Launceston Down to Little Down

A few yards after a holly tree in the hedge on your right, the track comes out onto a wide intersection with a track on your left between the field fence and another mixed wood. The field on your right has dropped into a steep corner and, past its hedge, a grassy, scrub-strewn patch harbours a support for overhead electric wires. Looking back, you will see Bridleway arrows on both gate posts on the corner of the fenced field.

Keep straight on, slightly downwards and with tangled coppiced hazels on your right for nearly 1/2 mile. On the way, the track bends a bit as it passes a large, wire fenced and grass covered water tank in the field on the left (watch out for the manhole covers in your path). Now, when you arrive at a wide junction of the Bridleway where a firm, grassless track comes up from your left, turn right with the coppiced hazels still on the RH corner and a hedge facing you. There are two Bridleway arrows on the LH corner but these are of purely academic interest. Follow the wide farm track to a cantilever gate across the path and, through the gate, take the Bridleway which goes round to the left - not the descending one known as Turners Lane which goes down to Tarrant Monkton. I know "The Langton Arms" is a most inviting hostelry, with good food and fine beer, but it's too early isn't it.

So, stiffen those sinews and keep going - You've hardly done 1.1/2 miles. Keep going, on a wide, level, grassy track with a thick hedge on the left and a fence and hedge on the right. The track begins to descend fractionally and, at a gap in the RH hedge, there are fine views along the Tarrant Valley, Just after this gap, the track appears to be sunken but the field on the left is high and the fence on the right is banked above the level of the field. Emerging into a wide, grassy area with an embankment on the left and with the fence veering away to the right, the grass track which descends on the right goes down to (or comes back up from) Tarrant Monkton. This grassy lane is known as Common Drove.

Could it be that this high level track is a remnant of a minor drovers' road, similar to the Salisbury Way and the Ox Drove?

The signpost by the fence on the left points back to "Turners Lane 1/2" whilst the Bridleway arrow on the post next to the cantilever gate directs you onwards. Beyond the gate, as the track resumes normal width, a gate into the field on your left leads to a signed Bridleway which crosses the field, passing a dead tree in the middle. However, keep going on this high, straight and grassy track, still enjoying the views into the Tarrant valley down on your right.

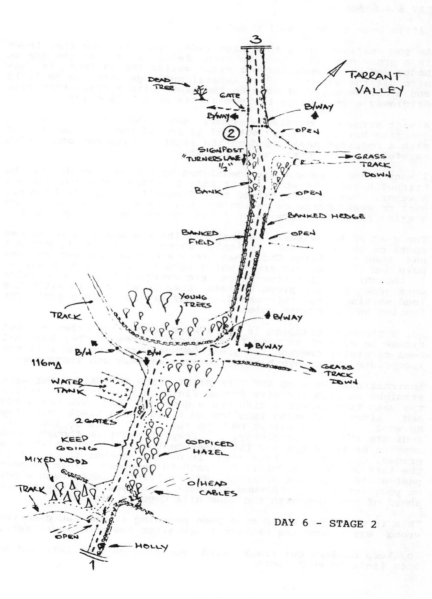

TARRANT VALLEY

3

DEAD TREE

GATE
B/WAY
B/WAY

② OPEN

SIGNPOST
"TURNERS LANE ½"

GRASS TRACK DOWN

BANK

OPEN

BANKED HEDGE

BANKED FIELD

OPEN

OPEN

YOUNG TREES

TRACK

B/WAY

B/H
B/W

B/WAY

116m△

GRASS TRACK DOWN

WATER TANK

2 GATES

KEEP GOING

COPPICED HAZEL

MIXED WOOD

O/HEAD CABLES

TRACK

DAY 6 – STAGE 2

OPEN

HOLLY

1

141

DAY 6 - STAGE 3

Little Down to Dean Hill Coppice

As you continue along this high lane, you will see that there
is a great deal of expensive iron fence in amongst the sparse
hedge and wire fence on your right whilst the LH fence is just
wire all the way. Past several openings into the RH field
and a narrow strip of wood on the right with confirmation blue
Bridleway arrows close by, you arrive at a T-junction.

A vast array of Bridleway arrows adorn the gateposts at this
junction but turn sharp left and go around the cantilever gate
with a coppiced hazel wood on the right. Stop now and listen
carefully to the next instructions:

I went wrong here and was admonished by the Head Warden of the
Crichel Estate, to whom all of this farmland and woods belong.
However, having ascertained that I wasn't a complete bounder,
bent on destruction or evildoing, he very kindly settled a few
queries about forestry which I had amassed on the Day's walk.

The gist of his answers is that: a) The red and yellow painted
spots on the fir trees indicate which are to be thinned out
and when : b) Large Christmas trees are grown for papermaking
pulp and : c) The fir trees which lose their needles in winter
(I thought that all pine trees were evergreen) are larch which
were grown for pit props because they never gave in without a
loud warning crack beforehand. They are now mainly grown for
fencing and telegraph poles.

So, accidental trespass is not always a shooting offence, but
please be careful to keep to my guided routes. They have all
been carefully checked, at great personal risk as you will now
appreciate, to ensure harmony between walkers and landowners.

Instructions are - DO NOT TURN RIGHT AFTER THE GATE - but keep
straight on with the wire fenced field on your left. Follow
the main track where a side route goes off left into the woods
and, after an opening into the LH field and a track into the
RH wood, the blue arrows next to the field gate on the left
indicate the main Bridleway. Keep straight on though, with
coppice on the right and fir trees on the left, and start on a
gradual descent. Past open fields and another track off to
the left which is a Public Footpath to Manswood, keep on down
past a wider section of track and a turning into young woods
on your left. Around the next bend, you will see a barn
ahead of you, opposite the Dean Hill Coppice Pig Farm.

This is where you would have been emerging if you had gone the
wrong way - down the Private track after the cantilever gate.

So, keep on down our track, with woodland on your left and an
open field on your right.

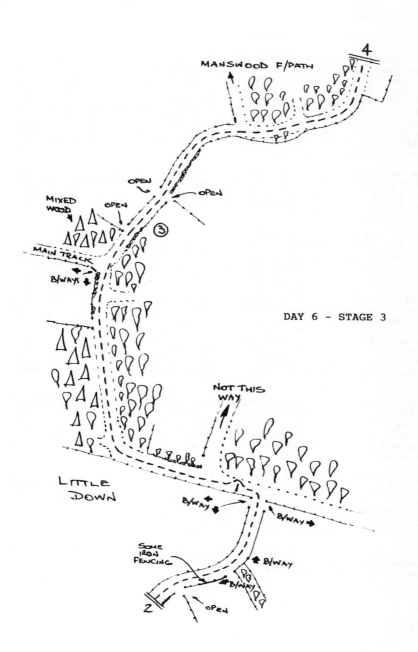

MANSWOOD F/PATH

4

OPEN

OPEN

OPEN

MIXED WOOD

OPEN

③

MAIN TRACK

B/WAYS

DAY 6 - STAGE 3

NOT THIS WAY

LITTLE DOWN

B/WAY

B/WAY

SOME IRON FENCING

B/WAY

B/WAY

2

OPEN

DAY 6 - STAGE 4

Dean Hill Coppice to Hemsworth Farm

Past the Private track on your right and the LH track past the
high-fenced coppice, you now pass a large barn on your right
and a collection bay on the left. The woodland on the left is
Dean Hill Coppice which now houses the Pig Rearing Unit, from
where intermittent argumentative squeals are frequently heard.
Keep on down, with the Coppice on your left and a wire-fenced
field on your right, to an opening into this RH field and a
hedged grassy track next to it. A faded yellow arrow on the
corner, almost in the hedge, shows that this is a Footpath but
you don't need it, anyway.

Keep on the main track, now with grass verges and wire fences
on both sides, to the LH corner of the coppiced trees where a
farm track, and an unsigned Public Footpath, goes up to Dean
Farm Dairy. If you're lucky, you won't meet the cattle en
route along your Bridleway.

As you follow the straight track, on the distant horizon, you
will see Badbury Rings. It's the open-wooded area next to a
more dense wood to its left, far away over the fields. The
deeper wood is King Down, through which you will pass on your
way to the hill fort and your ultimate destination, Wimborne
Minster, 8 miles from here. Past the Dairy turning and
a cattle trough in the field on the right, continue down the
track with a hedge now on your left. Another track comes
in from your right where, on my last visit to the area, a lone
and sorrowful looking cow came ambling down - clearly left
behind when the rest were herded to the milking parlour, but
determined to get there, in her own time. After two more
troughs in opposing fields, the wide, grass verge on the next
corner leads to a wide, grassy Footpath which goes up between
fields on your left.

Keep straight on, passing the brick and flint Dean Farmhouse
on the left with its associated buildings and farmyard in the
corner. Following the curving track between fenced fields,
the low LH field and the hedged RH field bring you to the exit
onto the Witchampton Road. A plethora of signs gives you
something to read on the corners.

You are now told that this is Crichel Farm Estate, including
Dean Hill Coppice and Dean Farm Dairy, (but you already knew
that). You are further informed that the "Bridleway" leads
to "A354 Rd 3.3/4" and to "Manswood 2.1/2". Another Bridleway
sign, broken and lost in the grass verge when I came this way
last, should point across the road to "Badbury Rings 2.1/2".

Cross over the grass-verged road and go into the driveway of
"Hemsworth Farm", home of the "Famous Shapwick Flock", with
fields on both sides of the drive.

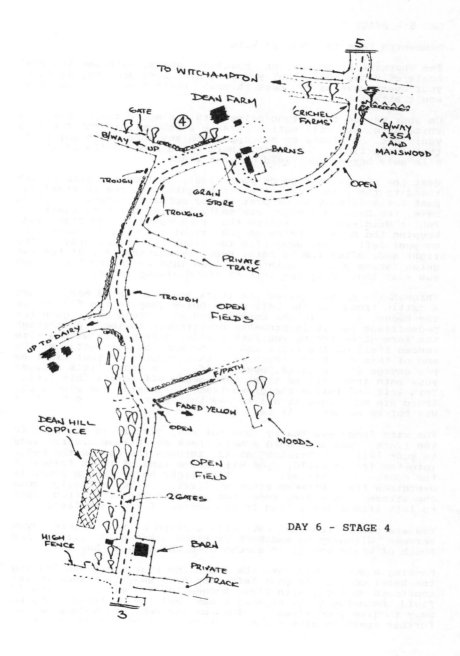

TO WITCHAMPTON

DEAN FARM

5

'CRICHEL FARMS'

'B/WAY
A354
AND
MANSWOOD

OPEN

GATE

④

B/WAY

UP

BARNS

TROUGH

GRAIN
STORE

TROUGHS

PRIVATE
TRACK

TROUGH

OPEN
FIELDS

UP TO DAIRY

F/PATH

FADED YELLOW

DEAN HILL
COPPICE

OPEN

WOODS.

OPEN
FIELD

2 GATES

HIGH
FENCE

BARN

PRIVATE
TRACK

DAY 6 - STAGE 4

3

DAY 6 - STAGE 5

Hemsworth Farm to Bradford Path

The Shapwick Flock are the roundest sheep, with the thickest
coats of dense wool, that you have ever seen and they'll watch
your every move as you pass through their homeland - but they
won't attack.

On your way up the tarmac drive with the speed ramps, past the
white gate, you will notice strange earthworks in the field on
your left.   These do not appear on any maps or in any books
that I can find.   However, there was a Roman Villa about 1/2
mile away beyond the field on your right.

Past the hedged cottage on your right, follow the drive/track
round to the left, past the corner gate into the LH field and
past the Bridleway arrow post in the opposite verge.   From
here, the Bridleway signs are sadly lacking but this really is
Public Bridleway.   Follow the track round to the right and,
keeping the mass of barns on your right and with a single barn
on your left , bear away from the track which runs away to the
right and, after the LH barn, head towards the left of the two
gates facing you.   Both gates lead into adjoining fields and
you want the one to the left of the dividing hedge.

Through the gate, follow the track against the RH hedge, past
a cattle trough on the left and a horse jump in the far end of
the hedge.   In the corner, you will see a small gate for
pedestrians but it is probably overgrown. Instead, go through
the farm gates facing you into a wide, grassy area with a wire
fenced field on the right and a pine wood on the left. At the
end of this clearing, there is a thin coppice on your right as
you emerge into a large, open field.   A grass track crosses
your path from left to right and heads off across this field.
Turn left and follow the green track alongside the pine wood.
There are no signs at all to say that this is Public Right of
Way but be assured - it is.

The wire fence eventually runs out and, just round the bend in
the track, you come onto a main track which runs clearly away
to your left.   Straight ahead, through the gap in the hedge
into the facing field, you will see a line of trees following
the course of a stream.   Turn right here, into a possibly
overgrown track between trees at first.   You actually cross
the stream, in a pipe under the path, as it flows from right
to left from a small pond in the corner of the last field.

You are now on the last navigable section of the Ackling Dyke
between Witchampton and Badbury Rings - and only 1.1/2 miles
South of where you first encountered the Dyke on Day 1.

Passing a horse jump into the field on your right and leaving
the hazel coppice on your left, the Bridleway (for such it is)
continues upwards, with close hedges for 1/2 mile, with the LH
field becoming quite high at times and the RH field dropping
away to give good views.   Towards its end, the hedges become
further apart to give easier walking - out of the horse ruts.

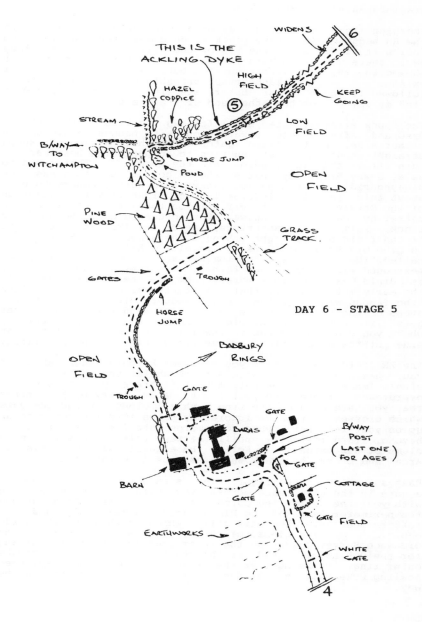

THIS IS THE
ACKLING DYKE

WIDENS

6

HIGH
FIELD

KEEP
GOING

HAZEL
COPPICE

⑤

STREAM

LOW
FIELD

B/WAY
TO
WITCHAMPTON

UP

HORSE JUMP

POND

OPEN
FIELD

PINE
WOOD

GRASS
TRACK.

GATES

TROUGH

DAY 6 - STAGE 5

HORSE
JUMP

BADBURY
RINGS

OPEN
FIELD

TROUGH

GATE

GATE

B/WAY
POST
(LAST ONE)
FOR AGES)

BARNS

BARN

GATE

GATE

COTTAGE

GATE

FIELD

EARTHWORKS

GATE

WHITE
GATE

4

147

DAY 6 - STAGE 6

Bradford Path to Badbury Rings

Emerging from the wide, grassy Bridleway, with a horse jump in
the RH hedge, join a farm track which comes from your left and
follow it slowly up to the top of the hill.   Not very long
ago, there was a Footpath yellow arrow on this gatepost which
showed the way to Tarrant Rushton but, sadly, this no longer
exists.   Its disappearance probably explains why, when I
followed it about a year before its final demise, I couldn't
find my way out of the other end of the field.

The track straight ahead still follows the line of the Ackling
Dyke and, after a long, upward slope with hedges and verges on
either side, and two field gates about half way up, it keeps
straight on at the first junction to go past King Down Farm.
Turn off to the right, here, into the woods.   There used to
be a 3-way Bridleway post on the LH corner but that has now
disappeared.   Then again, I have told Dorset County Council
about this (and the singular lack of signs from the junction
of the Bridleways and the Witchampton road) so it could all be
better by now.   Anyway, having turned onto the woodland
track, follow its meanderings, never far from the wire fence
of the field on the right, through the woods.   Ronald Good
in "The Old Roads of Dorset" recalls that these old woods,
called "The Oaks", are "of immense age, bowed and hollow, and
festooned with lichens and ferns".   They are known locally
as "Druid Oaks" but this merely confirms their great age.   In
the early 16th Century, that great traveller Leland visited
"the famous wood of Bathan, near Badbury Rings.   So, in the
steps of the famous, follow the tangled wood past a cantilever
gate into a field on the right, across a junction of tracks,
where you need to zig-zag to the left, to emerge on the other
side of the woods onto a grassy track between fenced fields.

The LH field, over which you can see Badbury Rings ahead of
you, has a hedge and a double fence whilst the RH field has a
single fence.   At the bottom of this track, past a gated and
overgrown shrubbery on your right, a Bridleway post confirms
that you have been on the true path all along.   Round the gate
which crosses your path, ignore any paths into the dense scrub
up on your left but, when you emerge onto the grassier slopes
beyond, turn instantly uphill between this dense scrub and a
clump of hawthorns.   Follow the edge of this "Conservation
Area" and cross the track which emerges from the gate.

Past a tumulus on the right, keep straight on up the slope to
a gate in the wire fence across your path. If you have a dog
with you, the notice indicates that you will heve to go around
the perimeter fence of the Rings, join the main B3082 and turn
left to meet us at the exit stile which is shown on the guide
map.   If dogless, climb over the gate and look for the
Ordnance Survey column on the inner ring to your left.   Aiming
for the O S column, head for the staircase up the slope of the
outer ring, crossing over the track which is the re-aligned
Ackling Dyke route to Maiden Castle, near Dorchester, on the
way.

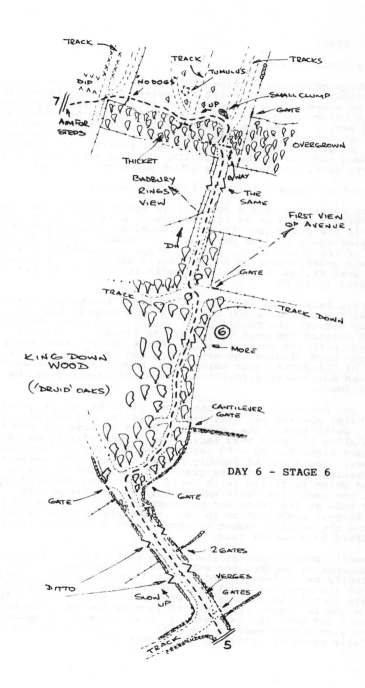

TRACK

TRACK

TRACKS

TUMULUS

V V V
DIP
^ ^ ^

NO DOGS

SMALL CLUMP

GATE

7 //
AIM FOR
STEPS

8 UP

OVERGROWN

THICKET

BADBURY
RINGS
VIEW

B'WAY

THE
SAME

FIRST VIEW
OF AVENUE.

DN

GATE

TRACK

TRACK DOWN

⑥

MORE

KING DOWN
WOOD

('DRUID' OAKS)

CANTILEVER
GATE

DAY 6 – STAGE 6

GATE

GATE

2 GATES

VERGES

DITTO

GATES

SLOW
UP

TRACK

5

DAY 6 - STAGE 7

Badbury Rings to B3082

To reduce excessive erosion of this important Stone-age site, the National Trust have built a series of inconspicuous steps into the slopes and I implore you to treat your approach to the O S column as a maze and to use all of the staggered steps on the way. The map shows that the most direct route over the rings actually leads away from the O S column, towards the right, so go that way and double back towards the column when you reach the top of the inner ring. Enjoy the feel of this historic site, appreciate the views and take your time.

Lean on the column, it's time for a few details:

Badbury Rings encloses a space of 14 acres whilst the central ring, with a depth of 40 ft, measures 1 mile in circumference. Built in the Stone-age, it was occupied successively by Bronze age, Iron-age and Saxon settlers. Named after Bada, local chief of the Durotriges, Badbury Rings succumbed to the Roman invaders under Vespasian in the early days of the invasion of South-West England which started with the fall of Vectis (Isle of Wight) in AD 45.

Now, turn back along the inner ring for a few yards, then turn towards the centre, along the grass path between the old oaks. Head up between the fenced pine enclosures to the information plinth marking the dead centre of the Rings. The plinth is aligned with its corners facing North, South, East and West. When you have studied the map on top and tried to pick out the parts of Cranborne Chase which you have visited, between the East and North-West directions, leave the plinth down the line of due South.

When you arrive on top of the inner ring, study the grassland down below you and you will see a definite, and ancient, grass track which leaves the Rings and heads towards the avenue of trees along the main road facing you. Keep this track in mind and turn right for 50 - 60 yards along the top of the ring for the best route out of Badbury Rings, using steps where these are available. On the green track, follow it across open ground which is filled with mole hills and hawthorn bushes until you reach the fence which encloses the Rings site. The track ends at the fence but go over the stile about 10 yards away to your right out on to an immensely wide verge between you and the ancient avenue of beech trees which line the B3082 Blandford to Wimborne road.

The small beech trees in the frames will replace the existing avenue when it becomes too expensive to preserve. They are constantly being treated and pruned by tree surgeons and the cost to the National Trust must be enormous. However, I'm certain they'll be with us for many years yet. Turn left and follow the LH verge, past the RH turning towards Sturminster Marshall and past the car parking area where 1.1/2 gates lead onto a signed Bridleway on the left. After the car park, carefully cross the B3082 at its safest point.

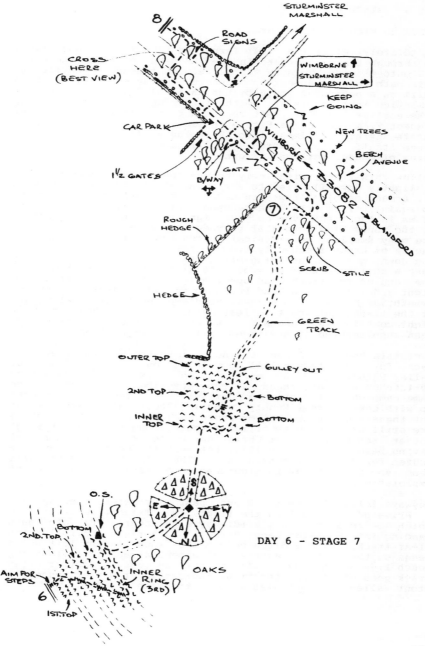

DAY 6 - STAGE 7

DAY 6 - STAGE 8

B3082 to Kingston Lacy Park

Immediately after the "Left Turn" and "200 Yards" road signs, go through the wooden gate in the RH hedge off the wide verge and onto a wide, grassy track between fenced, open fields. This path doesn't appear on Ordnance Survey maps but has been built as a permanent route by the National Trust.   Oh! didn't I mention that nearly all of the land since you joined Ackling Dyke earlier today was left to the National Trust under a vast bequest from the Bankes Estate in 1985?   Well, the 7000 acre estate stretches almost into Wimborne whilst Kingston Lacy House itself,   around which you will soon be passing, has 250 acres of wooded park on its own.

Follow this track, pleasantly between new fenced hedges and on a slightly downhill lie, to a zig-zag at the bottom.   After a dip around an older hawthorn hedge, the track begins to climb up again.   From here, the cacophony of sound from the arguing crows in the trees over on your right is a timely introduction to the usual bird song that pervades the Park itself.   There are many smaller, more musical, birds around here but the loud cackle of crows frequently drowns their songs.   Anyway, up and down, past an intruding bit of hedge on the way up, you go past a replanted wood on your left at the top of the rise.   At the end of the track, an opening leads into the field on the right and 1.1/2 gates lead you onto an old Bridleway known as Sweetbriar Drove.   A 3-way Bridleway post points along all of the tracks but you turn left here.   The hedge on your right contains many beeches, oaks and ash trees but these have been supplemented by new trees, still in timber frames.

Over this hedge, you can look down into the Stour valley.   In fact, for 3/4 mile you will be walking on part of "The Stour Valley Path", the '60 miles in 5 days' guided walk from Christchurch to Stourhead which I described in my book of the same name which I mentioned earlier.   You will soon meet up with some Dorset County Council "Stour Valley Way" signs but these are not part of my route.   In 1995 Dorset Council are still working on an official route along the Stour through Dorset, the section from Christchurch to Sturminster Marshall having been completed in 1994, but we both decided on separate routes for different reasons and "The Stour Valley Path" will lead you all the way to Stourhead on a fascinating journey of exploration.

Anyway, follow Sweetbriar Drove, past many gates, openings and a "Private" track off to the right, to a T-junction at its end which bears a three-way Bridleway sign near a "Private" gate leading into Kingston Lacy Park.   Turn right and follow the clear track, with a ditch before the woods on the left and a hedge on the right, negotiating a bend around an overhanging beech tree on the way.   At the next LH corner, another green track goes off right, the first indication of Dorset Council's Stour Valley Way, but just keep to the main track.

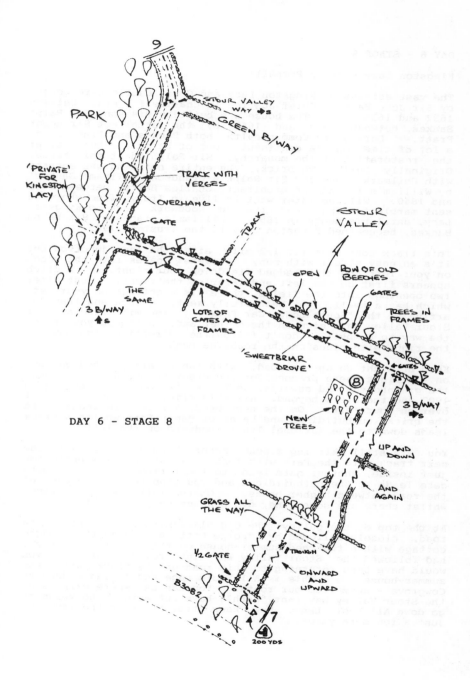

9

PARK

STOUR VALLEY WAY ➔s

GREEN B/WAY

'PRIVATE' FOR KINGSTON LACY

TRACK WITH VERGES

OVERHANG.

GATE

TRACK

STOUR VALLEY

3 B/WAY ➔s

THE SAME

LOTS OF GATES AND FRAMES

OPEN

ROW OF OLD BEECHES

GATES

TREES IN FRAMES

'SWEETBRIAR DROVE'

GATES ➔s R

⑧

3 B/WAY ➔s

DAY 6 - STAGE 8

NEW TREES

UP AND DOWN

AND AGAIN

GRASS ALL THE WAY

½ GATE

TROUGH

ONWARD AND UPWARD

B3082

△ 7

🔵 200 YDS

DAY 6 - STAGE 9

Kingston Lacy Park to Pamphill

The vast estates of Kingston Lacy and Corfe Castle were bought by Sir John Bankes, Chief Justice in Charles I's era, between 1632 and 1635. The house was built by his son, Sir Ralph Bankes, between 1663 and 1665 by the architect Sir Roger Pratt. During the Commonwealth, both Bankes and Pratt spent a lot of time on the continent, out of harms way but, after the restoration of the monarchy, Sir Ralph built this house. Originally built with brick, the entire building was encased with Chilmark stone for Sir Ralph's grandson, William Bankes' by William's friend and architect, Charles Barry, between 1835 and 1840. William later went to live in Italy, from where he sent marble fittings and Italian woodwork back to Kingston Lacy, until his death in 1855. William's grandson, Sir Ralph Bankes, bequeathed Kingston Lacy to the Trust in 1985.

This track continues for 1/2 mile after the last junction but it's an easy stroll with many "Private" gates into the woods on your left and with hedged fields on your right. A ditch appears first on the left and later on the right. Just after two openings into the fields, there is a cottage on your left which has a small, but beautifully kept, garden and then you arrive at the "South Lodge Car Park". You will find another Stour Valley Way sign on the corner and, although you are on the way to Pamphill, don't follow the direction sign down to the right with pines on the roadside bank.

Keep straight on up the road, with the ornately-gated gardens on the right where produce for the great house was grown, past the greenhouses and onwards, next past two more cottages dated 1907 and the field beyond. All this time, the woods are still over on your left. On the next bend, a farm gate leads up to the brick outbuildings and barns of Manor Farm whilst a track leads down to the National Trust woodyard on the left.

You are still skirting around Manor Farm and, opposite the next track into the Park with fences, a gate and low buildings just inside, another gate leads to the farmhouse. One more gate leads to the outbuildings and you then begin an ascent of the road between higher banks. On the left are two cottages whilst there are some fine, old oaks up on your right.

At the top of the gulley, the old blacksmith's forge abuts the road, closely followed by "Forge Cottage" and another hedged cottage with a thatched summer-house on the corner. If you had followed the Stour Valley Way sign from the car park, you would have been returning to this road up the track after the summer-house. This is All Fools Lane and it leads down to Cowgrove - away from our route. You can see where walkers on the Stour Valley Way (not "Path") have cut across the verge to go down All Fools Lane. Now, keep straight on up the lane for just a few more yards.

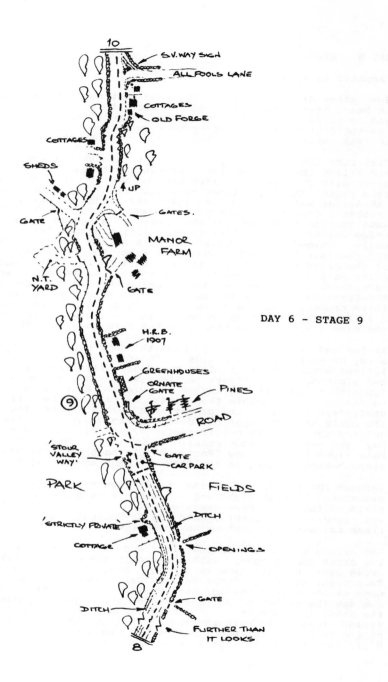

DAY 6 - STAGE 9

DAY 6 - STAGE 10

Pamphill to River Stour

Just after All Fools Lane, the road continues around a slight
LH bend, past the white-gated entrance to St Stephen's Church
and on to Pamphill Dairy Farm Shop. You can get a nice cup of
tea there or a snack to bring back with you if you would like
to rest awhile by the cricket pitch. However, I digress.

Just past the field gate, turn right through the wooden posts
and follow the straggly path through the trees. Cross a small
ditch with the sleeper bridge and you will be in a car parking
area signed "National Trust Pamphill Green". This wonderful
Oak Avenue was planted in 1846 and leads straight to St
Stephen's Church. However, this wasn't built until 1907, the
same year as those two cottages which you passed after "South
Lodge Car Park". Over on your left are some farm cottages
whilst, beyond the car park, there is a fine thatched cottage
and the late 17th Century Pamphill Manor House lies at the end
of the elevated track from the car park to its hedged gardens.
Carry on along the grass to the right of the Avenue. Why not
have a short rest on the bench beneath the old oak tree facing
the thatched 1909 cricket pavilion. On a late summer evening,
there probably isn't a better place to be in all England, with
a village cricket match drawing to its close - especially if
you have a little something from the Farm Shop to nibble on.

At the end of the Avenue, go past the anti-car barriers and an
array of gates on the RH side. Follow the road past Pamphill
Village School, built in 1698 by Roger Gillingham as a school
and almshouse. After the Stour Valley Way marker which is
opposite a lane turning across the Green, skirt around the LH
bushes and, just before the first cottage on Vine Hill, turn
sharp left and cross the grassy area to the electricity pylon.
You could keep straight on down the road but your chances of
getting run over are considerable - and, if you go the pretty
way, you may see a woodpecker or some jays. Under the pylon,
bear right by the 3-way "Footpath" signpost and drop down some
steps between bushes to the first of many squeeze-stiles.

Through the stile, follow the path down to the left, with an
embankment on your right and a few trees, a ditch and a fenced
field on the left. More steps bring you to a junction of paths
and, ignoring all others, take the RH Footpath, along a row of
trees and with the bank up on your right.

The stream runs along on your left and, after the next stile,
you cross open ground, with a wooden fence on your right, to
cross over this stream with a plank bridge and another stile.
Turn right after the Stour Valley Way signpost and follow the
edge of the stream through this field. Straight ahead, you
can see the arches of Julians Bridge, the medieval crossing of
the Stour to Wimborne. Over the stile at the end of the
field, turn right onto the road, then go over the next stile
on the left with the Stour Valley Way signpost, opposite Vine
Hill, into the field with a hedge and ditch on your left.

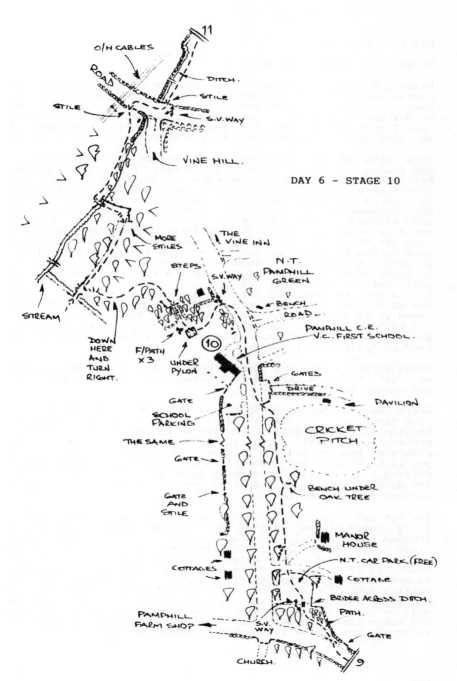

DAY 6 - STAGE 10

O/H CABLES

ROAD

DITCH.

STILE

STILE

S.V. WAY

VINE HILL.

MORE STILES

THE VINE INN

STEPS

S.V. WAY

N.T. PAMPHILL GREEN

BENCH

ROAD

STREAM

PAMPHILL C.E. V.C. FIRST SCHOOL.

DOWN HERE AND TURN RIGHT.

F/PATH x 3

UNDER PYLON

(10)

GATES

DRIVE

PAVILION

GATE

SCHOOL PARKING

THE SAME

GATE

CRICKET PITCH.

GATE AND STILE

BENCH UNDER OAK TREE

MANOR HOUSE

N.T. CAR PARK (FREE)

COTTAGES

COTTAGE

BRIDGE ACROSS DITCH.

PATH.

PAMPHILL FARM SHOP

S.V. WAY

GATE

CHURCH.

9

DAY 6 - STAGE 11

River Stour to Wimborne Minster

Heading towards the River, cross over the stream, using the LH
signed footbridge and the squeeze-stile.   In this next field,
keep following the wide grass path to the next stile and the
bridge across a ditch.   On the River bank, there is the most
magnificent willow with long branches gracefully hanging from
its vast bulk.   I wonder how many cricket bats it would make?

Keep straight on, ignoring a path bearing off to your left,
and follow the short fence to the corner of the facing hedge,
beyond which a singularly unused stile stands at the end of a
broken wire fence.   With the fence on your left, and football
pitches on its other side, go past a fenced rainwater outfall
and, between hawthorns and a few small trees, you emerge into
some allotments with a track coming from your left.   Aim for
the Minster which you will see directly ahead of you and don't
turn off the track at all.   At its end, a Footpath sign points
back to Eye Bridge, just past where you came across the field
to join the River.   When you come onto a tarmac road with
a block of flats on the right, follow the road around to the
left, between townhouses and garages, past the Pay and Display
Car Park on the left and the Printers on the right.   In a
few yards, you reach the main B3082 Wimborne to Blandford road
where it is still called Victoria Road.   There is another Pay
Car Park on the left corner of Old Road as you leave it.   Now,
be very careful. Wimborne is usually very busy and you're not
used to traffic at the moment.

Cross Victoria Road and turn up West Street, past the "Pudding
and Pye" on the corner, past a garage and several small shops
and houses along the road.

Where the road bends around to the left, turn into the lane on
your right.   Just ahead is the old Wesleyan Chapel and,
bearing left and right, you arrive in Cornmarket.   In this
pedestrianized area, close to the "White Hart Inn", there are
plenty of benches but you're nearly there now.   Just ahead of
you is Cooks Row and you will recall that this is where Day 1
started, so stroll nonchalently into Cooks Row and turn onto
the Minster path where the glass door of the North Transept is
waiting to welcome you back.

The Minster church of St Cuthburga is built on the site of the
Abbey Church of the earlier Benedictine nunnery which was
founded about AD 713. Of special interest is the astronomical
clock on the South wall inside the West tower.   On the North
wall, you can see the Quarter Jack ring the bells by his side
every 1/4 of an hour.   He is dressed as a Grenadier Guard and
is connected to the Orrery clock inside.   The Minster is well
worth a special visit and, if you would like to find out more
about the Saxon chest, the Chained Library, the Man in the
Wall or the Uvedale Monument, you should return another day
and spend some time with the "Guide for Pilgrims and Visitors"
which you can buy at the Minster's bookshop.

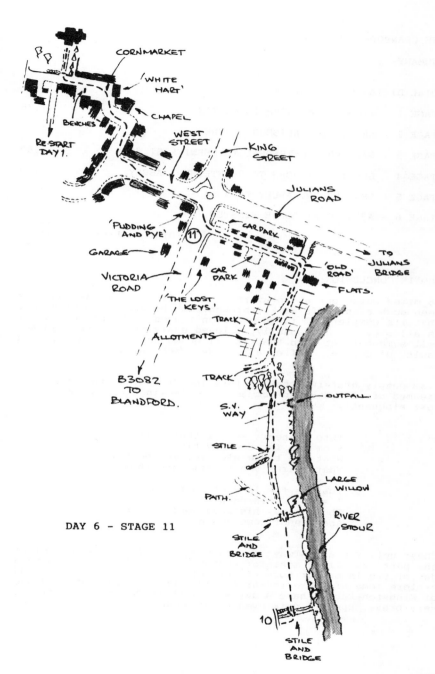

CORNMARKET

'WHITE HART'

CHAPEL

BENCHES

RESTART DAY 1.

WEST STREET

KING STREET

JULIANS ROAD

CAR PARK

'PUDDING AND PYE'

⑪

GARAGE

VICTORIA ROAD

CAR PARK

'OLD ROAD'

TO JULIANS BRIDGE

FLATS.

'THE LOST KEYS'

TRACK

ALLOTMENTS

B3082 TO BLANDFORD.

TRACK

OUTFALL.

S.V. WAY

STILE

LARGE WILLOW

PATH.

RIVER STOUR

DAY 6 - STAGE 11

STILE AND BRIDGE

10

STILE AND BRIDGE

159

THE CRANBORNE CHASE PATH

SUMMARY

TOTAL DISTANCES (in miles):

STAGE 1 - WIMBORNE MINSTER TO MARTIN -	17.75
STAGE 2 - MARTIN TO SALISBURY CATHEDRAL -	11
STAGE 3 - SALISBURY CATHEDRAL TO BERWICK ST JOHN -	15.50
STAGE 4 - BERWICK ST JOHN TO SHAFTESBURY ABBEY -	8.50
STAGE 5 - SHAFTESBURY ABBEY TO A354 -	12
STAGE 6 - A354 TO WIMBORNE MINSTER -	11.25
TOTAL MILEAGE:	76

AND IN CONCLUSION:

76 miles works out at an average of 12.67 miles a Day and it's
been such a splendid walk, through such beautiful countryside,
that its completion is an occasion tinged with sorrow that it
is all over.   Personally, I loved every step of the way and
felt somewhat let down that it all ended so soon.   All my own
fault, of course.   After all, I designed the walk.

I am deeply grateful that, before The Cranborne Chase Path was
dreamed of, A E Housman summed up my feelings at journey's end
most eloquently:

> Into my heart an air that kills
> From yon far country blows:
> What are those blue remembered hills,
> What spires, what farms are those?
>
> That is the land of lost content,
> I see it shining plain,
> Those happy highways where I went
> And cannot come again.

Cheer up! You can always go round again, of course, or select
the parts you liked most for another visit. You could spend a
day or two in one or more of our three corner towns, visit and
explore some of the earthworks sites, go back to Chettle House
or Kingston Lacy, have a day at Salisbury Races - or, for the
very brave, spend a dark evening at Washers Pit.

THE CRANBORNE CHASE PATH

ACKNOWLEDGMENTS:

First, I would like to thank Mr C Burt, Marketing Officer for Wilts and Dorset Bus Company for his assurances that the bus routes and numbers used in this book are secure.

I would like to thank Mr W L Fisher of Wiltshire County Council and Mr Nash of Salisbury District Council, both from their respective Councils' Environmental Health Departments, for their assurances that the Drovers Road in the Salisbury Racecourse area will be kept clear of rubbish in future.

I would like to thank Mr R Webb of the Dorset County Council's Rights of Way Department for his help concerning missing signs and overgrown stiles in the Bradford Barrow and Hemsworth Farm areas whilst Mr Cook of North Dorset District Council has made sure that the two stiles after the bridge at Cann were renewed after the new fences were put in.

Most of all, I would like to thank my wife, Janet, for her help during my obsession with "The Cranborne Chase Path", for accompanying me on some of the Stages and for sending me off with suitable provisions and my bus fares.

The Avenue, Eastbury Park. Page 130

BIBLIOGRAPHY:

On completing this book, it came as a surprise to find exactly
how many books had provided me with so much information for my
little asides during the walk.   I gratefully acknowledge all
the help given by the Reference   Libraries of Dorset County
Council at The Lansdowne, Bournemouth and of Wiltshire County
Council at Salisbury.

Parliament Map, Wilts., 1773 by John Andrews and Andrew Dury.

Droving in Wiltshire by K G Watts for Wiltshire Life Society.

Hinerarium Curiosum, 1724 by William Stukely.

Neolithic Dew-Ponds and Cattle-Ways, 1905 by Arthur Hubbard
and George Hubbard.

Folklore and Witchcraft in Dorset and Wiltshire by J Chadwick.

Ancient Earthworks of Cranborne Chase, 1913 by Heywood Sumner.

Mysterious Dorset, 1987 by Rodney Legg.

Excavations in Cranborne Chase, 1887-98 by Lieutenant-General
Pitt-Rivers.

Dorset Barrows by Leslie Grinsell FSA.

Roman Dorset, 1984 by Bill Putnam.

Wiltshire, 1976 by Ralph Whitlock

Dorset - Upalong and Downalong, 1935 by W I members: Edited by
Marianne R Dacombe.

The Stour Valley Path, 1994 by Edward R Griffiths.

The Old Roads of Dorset, 1940 by Ronald Good.

A Chronicle of Cranborne and Cranborne Chase, 1841 by Thomas W
Wake-Smart.

Cranborne Chase, 1980 by Desmond Hawkins.

Anecdotes and History of Cranborne Chase, 1818 by Wm. Chafin.

History and Antiquities of the County of Dorset, 1861-64 by
Rev. John Hutchins.

Dorset Churches, 1976 by Sir Owen Morshead, Dorset Historic
Churches Trust.

Inventory of Historical Monuments in the County of Dorset,
1970 by H M S O.

Salisbury Cathedral Guide, 1976 by Pitkin Pictorials.

INDEX

Washers Pit. 120
Water Lane, B. St John. 90
Wedgwood, Josiah/Thomas. 128
Well Bottom. 122,124
Wessex Ridgeway. 94,98
West Borough, Wimborne. 10
West Harnham. 64,69,74
West Street, Wimborne. 10,158
West Wood. 109,118,120
Weymouth. 50
White Hart Inn. 158
Whitesheet Hill. 60,72,84,86
Wight, Isle of. 150
Wildlife Act. 4
Wilksworth Park. 12
Wilton. 52,56,60,62,69,76
Wimborne Minster. 9,22,158
Wimborne Pumping Station. 12
Wimborne St Giles. 38
Windmill Hill. 50
Wincombe Woods. 102
Win Green. 89,92,94,138
Winchester. 88,108
Winklebury Hill Fort. 90
Winnie the Pooh. 86
Witchampton.18,20,122,144,146
Witchampton Abbey. 22
Witchampton Manor House. 22
Wordsworth, Bishop John. 70
Wyke Down. 34,36
Wykeham, William de. 88
Wylye, River. 64

Zouche, Abbess Elizabeth. 106